THE REVIVE CAFE COOKBOOK

www.revive.co.nz

Copyright © Revive Concepts Limited 2011
Published by Revive Concepts Limited
First printing 2011. Second printing 2012. Third printing 2012

ISBN 978-0-473-19057-6

Produced in New Zealand
Recipe Photography & Food Styling: Jeremy Dixon
Graphic Design: Rebecca Zwitser & Jeremy Dixon
Food Preparation: Jeremy Dixon, Maggi Foldi, Ricardo Delgado
Recipe testing and proofing: Verity Dixon, Nyree Tomkins, Ashlee Panton, Estelle & Dean Edwards, Brenda Wood, Keryn McCutcheon, Althea Hanna, Jo Pater, Heather Cameron, Dawn Simpson, Kjirstnne Jensen, Megan Tooley, Dyanne Dixon

Thank you to my chefs Nora Arama, Sue Knight, Nanik Widayani and Maggie Foldi for their help in developing and improving Revive's recipes over the years.
I would like to acknowledge David Davies, Joanne Davies, Stephen Davies, Annette Barlow and Adrian Davies for their invaluable support and expertise. Sadly, David Davies passed away shortly before the printing of this book.
I am indebted to David who believed in my vision for Revive from its inception and encouraged me to pursue my dream.

The publisher makes no guarantee as to the availability of the products in this book. Every effort has been made to ensure the accuracy of the information presented and any claims made; however, it is the responsibility of the reader to ensure the suitability of the product and recipe for their particular needs. Many natural ingredients vary in size and texture and differences in raw ingredients may marginally affect the outcome of some dishes. Most recipes have been adjusted from the cafe recipes to make them more appropriate for a home kitchen. All health advice given in this book is a guideline only. Professional medical or nutritional advice should be sought for any specific issues.

Metric and imperial measurements have been used in this cookbook. The tablespoon size used is 15ml (½fl oz), teaspoon 5ml ($^1/_6$fl oz) and cup 250ml (8fl oz). Some countries use slightly different sized measurements, however these will not make a significant difference to the outcome of the recipes.

Revive Cafes
16 Fort St, Auckland Central, New Zealand
33 Lorne St, Auckland Central, New Zealand

If you like the recipes in this book we recommend you sign up for the weekly inspirational Revive e-mails.
They contain a weekly recipe, cooking and lifestyle tips, the weekly Revive menu, special offers and Revive news.
Visit www.revive.co.nz to sign up or to purchase more copies of this book on-line.
Privacy Policy: Revive will never share your details and you can unsubscribe at any time
LIKE us on Facebook! www.facebook.com/cafe.revive.

the  revive cafe cookbook

Look after your body by making wise lifestyle decisions and you will look and feel amazing! It is a small investment for a massive return in your quality of life.

Contents

The Revive Story

In 2003 my wife, Verity, and I treated ourselves to a 10 day cleanse at a health retreat. We had steam baths, massages, days of juice fasting, long walks, nutritional education, cooking classes, naturopathic consultations and most importantly 10 days of rest. We came back with a newfound vitality and zest for life. By implementing simple changes in the ensuing months such as healthy eating, drinking plenty of water and exercise, we just felt so good!

While we were at the health retreat we learned some great tips on how to live a healthier lifestyle including how to cook healthy food. By feeding our bodies quality nutrients our body works as it should and life is so great!

Coming back to Auckland we realised that most cafes and eating places served food that was not really good for you. Sure muffins, pies, coffee, paninis and chips taste great, but soon afterwards you feel pretty lousy, not to mention the long term health issues that result.

I had a great career working for Sanitarium Health Food Company in Auckland for 10 years as a marketer of healthy breakfast cereals like Weet-Bix. I had always had the dream of becoming a chef or owning a cafe, so in late 2004 I took a bold and risky move and decided to leave my great job to open a healthy cafe.

I quickly faced some hard realisations in researching successful food outlets. In order to be successful in hospitality it appeared that you needed to serve coffee, alcohol, soft drinks, sugary cakes, food full of white flour and be open long hours in the weekends. Against the advice of several people, I decided that I could not sleep at night serving people these kinds of food and beverages, so I continued on in search of a suitable location.

I purchased an existing cafe that was not going that well on Fort St, literally signed my life away with a long term lease and over the Christmas holidays of 2004 I spent 2 months renovating, painting, organising and setting up my new cafe.

Thinking I knew it all from my Sanitarium career, I had to quickly learn the smarts of hospitality. It took a very stressful 12 months of menu amending, roster changing, marketing and staff training. However, I stuck at it, and eventually managed to get our formula working right. We had queues out the door most lunchtimes which made me very happy to know that so many people desired to eat heathy. It was a very intense 12 months, but the biggest thing I learned from this was to keep trying new things and to stick at it.

In 2008 I decided to take another big risk. We signed another lease and moved into a shop about 1 km up town in Lorne St. The site was previously a jeweller's shop. This was the perfect time to design a fresher cafe, and design it so it was operational and more efficient to run, with places for everything. We decided to cook the food for both shops in Fort St, and courier it up fresh every morning and afternoon. This formula worked very well.

I have a passion for sharing health principles with people. So many people are dragging themselves through life content with being overweight, having headaches, health issues and feeling tired all the time.

I put a lot of time into our weekly e-mails with health tips and recipes. I also do cooking demonstrations where I can share how simple it is to make healthy food. This cookbook is another way to share the recipes we use at Revive so people can learn how to prepare healthy meals themselves.

Jeremy Dixon, November 2011

Our Food Principles

At Revive we want food that is genuinely healthy, tasty and looking great, but not too different for mainstream people.

My objective was to get normal people eating healthier ... people who are currently eating the traditional western diet which would include meat, processed flour, sugars, pies, muffins, copious amounts of dairy, soft drinks and coffee.

The key differences of Revive food is as follows:

1. Use plenty of fresh produce.

2. Use whole grains like brown rice, quinoa, bulghur wheat and wholemeal flour which are significantly healthier than the processed grains found in most meals.

3. Use honey or date puree instead of processed and refined sugars.

4. Use a range of natural flavourings, herbs and spices and avoid black pepper and flavour enhancers.

5. Minimal use of dairy products, and only use soft cheeses (like feta and brie). Avoid the hard cheeses like cheddar and parmesan which are hard to digest.

6. Where possible combine whole grains with legumes/beans to form complete proteins. For example hotpots with chickpeas and brown rice.

7. Use fresh local produce so the menus are varied seasonally.

8. Instead of meat we use great protein sources such as chickpeas, beans, tofu, lentils and nuts.

9. Do not deep fry foods but use sparing amounts of rice bran oil as this is known to be better resistant to heat than other oils.

10. By nature of our healthy food, many dishes are gluten free. While there is nothing wrong with gluten in the diet, the western diet is full of it in highly refined wheat products which is why there are so many allergies.

11. Use free range eggs.

12. Instead of caffeine, alcohol or sugar based soft drinks we offer healthy juices, pure water and smoothies.

13. Avoid unhealthy additives like shrimp paste, cows rennet, flavour enhancers, and preservatives where possible.

While I respect that everyone will have their own food choices, I do want to ensure that when people come to Revive, they are nourished and leave with their body in better condition than when they arrived.

On the streets of the two Revive cafes there are more than 40 other eating outlets. (These outlets are virtually poisoning people with their food and beverages.) They mostly offer coffee, muffins, sweets and highly refined food that will damage peoples bodies, deplete their energy, vitality, quality of life and most likely shorten their lives.

I truly believe, and science backs it up, that if you put quality plant-based foods into your body you will have a very high chance of a long happy life full of vitality.

I hope this book may inspire you to eat healthy and have a pure lifestyle so you can enjoy a more energetic and quality life.

10 Revive Kitchen Tips

1. Get yourself a really good quality chef's knife (around 20cm/8in) and learn how to keep it sharp. Buy a small serrated knife as well. These are the only two knives you will ever need.

2. Stock your pantry with lots of lentils, nuts, grains, beans, spices and herbs. Buy in bulk and on special in advance which will not only save you time and money but will encourage you to use these healthy ingredients more often.

3. Fill your freezer with frozen vegetables, berries, pre-cooked beans and previously cooked meals.

4. Always think ahead. Using beans and whole grains is actually easy, but by pre-soaking & cooking your beans and pre-cooking your grains you can make meal times a breeze.

5. Have great flavour enhancers in your fridge like dressings, garlic puree, ginger puree and date puree so you can use at a moments notice.

6. Have an attitude of trying anything new. Step out of your cooking comfort zone. Be prepared for a few mistakes. If you stick to the recipes you will be fine.

7. Start with a clear, clean bench. Ten minutes clearing up before you start will save at least that in time when you are cooking.

8. Find a good produce store where you can buy good fresh vegetables. And find a good bulk store for spices, beans and other dry goods. Usually there is a good Asian and Indian grocery store in most neighbourhoods.

9. When you have cooked a dish make sure you taste it and check for saltiness, sweetness, flavours and texture. Many natural products and vegetables vary so some recipes need a little tweaking.

10. Save up for a good blender (tall, small blade and mixes liquids) and food processer (wide, S blade and can mix solids) which will open up many different techniques for cooking. Make sure you get the best you can. You are better off buying a high quality $800 food processor once in your life that works amazingly, than a $300 low quality one that will need replacing every 5 years. However, in the meantime a good stick blender will be adequate for most recipes and they are relatively inexpensive.

Cookbook Notes

Garlic, Ginger & Chilli

Garlic and ginger have amazing flavour enhancing properties and we use both extensively at Revive and in these recipes. You can just chop them up finely before adding to a dish or you can make your own purees by blending the garlic or ginger with a little oil.   You can buy pureed ginger at the supermarket and this is fine.   I recommend that garlic should always be used fresh and never purchased in a puree as it has an unpleasant flavour.   You can buy pre-crushed/pureed chilli in a jar which is used in some recipes (in small amounts).

Sweeteners

The recipes do not use added refined sugar. The most convenient sweetener is liquid honey. Alternatively make up a batch of date puree (page 154) which is an excellent and inexpensive sweetener to use. There are other healthy sweeteners available however, most tend to be quite expensive for everyday use.

Oils

My favourite oil is rice bran oil and is used extensively through these recipes. It is one of the best oils to cook with as it can withstand higher temperatures. Also, it has a very neutral taste so is good for dressings. Grape seed oil is also a good oil to use or you can use your favourite oil.

Beans/Chickpeas

I have used canned beans/chickpeas (garbanzo beans) in all of the recipes as this is the most convenient. However if you can use freshly cooked beans they will taste fresher. I recommend that you soak and cook your own beans and store them in your freezer. Simply run some hot water over them in a sieve or colander for 30 seconds to defrost.

Cooking Terms

Saute: to cook food on a high heat and in a little oil while stirring with a wooden spoon.
Simmer: to have food cooking at a low heat setting so it is just bubbling.
Roast: to bake in the oven covered with a little oil. Use the fan bake setting if your oven has one for more even cooking.

Quantities

The quantities for each dish are an estimate and will vary depending on cooking times and ingredient size. I have used one cup as an average serve size.

Mixing

You can mix most recipes in the pot you are cooking in or in a big mixing bowl. When mixing, it is important to stir gently so as not to damage the food. With salads, mix with your hands if possible. Gently lift up the ingredients and let them fall down with gravity rather than squeezing the ingredients.

Gluten Free & Dairy Free

A large proportion of the recipes are gluten free and/or dairy free. If you have any allergies you will need to check that each recipe is suitable and make adjustments as required.

If you are unhappy, sick, or not feeling fantastic, chances are that one or more of these principles are not happening in your life. Make a decision today to follow them all and to feel great all the time!

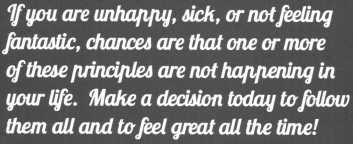

The 8 Keys to Healthy Living

Nutrition · Exercise · Water · Sunshine

Temperance · Air · Rest · Trust

These are the health principles that Revive is founded on.

If you apply these 8 simple steps in your day-to-day living, you will notice dramatic improvements in your vitality, health and quality of life.

Take responsibility for your health, make sure you use these principles every day and you will never regret it!

They are easy to remember. They spell "NEWSTART".

Please note that these are general lifestyle principles only and you are recommended to see a health professional regarding any serious health issues.

"You would not put bad fuel and oil into your car and expect good performance. You only have one body. Feed it well and you will live long and with vitality."

Nutrition

Fuel your body with quality food and feel great!

This is all about putting fresh, quality, alive foods into your body. Make sure a large proportion (ideally 50-70%) of your diet is fresh, raw fruit and vegetables.

Eat a variety of foods and cut down or eliminate animal products. Avoid fried and fatty foods. Eat whole grains rather than processed foods.

TIP: Eating slowly causes saliva to aid the digestion process which results in better absorption of vitamins and minerals and also less stress.

Exercise

Feel alive with 30 minutes of exercise per day!

Keeping active is a key requirement for good health. Your body needs at least 30 minutes of exercise three times per week.

Choose exercise that you enjoy. Try walking, running, cycling, squash, team sports, swimming, aerobics classes, tennis and commit to the ones you enjoy.

You need three types of exercise to be in peak condition: aerobic (e.g. running), resistance (e.g. weights) and stretching.

TIP: Arranging set times each week to exercise with a friend or spouse will make sure you do not miss out.

"People who cannot find time for exercise will have to make time for illness."

Water

Increase your vitality with 8 glasses of water a day!

Most people need 8 glasses (2 litres/ 2 quarts) of pure water a day. Tea, coffee, juice, flavoured waters do not count! However a non-caffeine herbal tea can be an occasional substitute.

Most people are dehydrated and do not know it and drinking water would transform their lives.

TIP: Have a sipper bottle with you all day. It will be beside you when you need it and you can make sure you are getting your 8 glasses a day.

TIP: Have 2 glasses of water with a squeeze of lemon first thing in the morning to help alkalize your body.

"Your body often confuses hunger with dehydration so if you feel hungry try a big glass of water first."

Sunshine

Enjoy the rejuvenating benefits of sunshine!

The sun has many healing and rejuvenating properties. You feel so good when you get some sunshine.

Experts believe we need at least 10 minutes of sun on the inside of our arms as a minimum per day!

TIP: If you are ever unwell or sick see what a difference half an hour out in the sun makes.

"The best way to get vitamin D is naturally from sunshine"

Temperance

All good things in moderation and set yourself free from harmful things!

We all know that drugs, cigarettes, caffeine and alcohol are bad for our health. Our bodies are much better off if we avoid them altogether!

Make wise choices for a body that can give you a long and prosperous life rather than choosing short term pleasures that lead to harmful results.

TIP: If you want to quit any bad habit you need the support and encouragement of a spouse or a close friend.

"When quitting something addictive you will find it easier if you exercise, eat healthy and drink lots of water."

"Get out in the forest, seaside or country regularly and deeply breathe in the fresh clean natural air."

Air

Breathe deeply to de-stress!

Good clean air is necessary for your body.

Breathe deeply and slowly. Many people are fast shallow breathers which does not allow your blood to get good oxygen.

The optimal number of breaths per minute is around 6 to 10. If you breathe faster than this you need to focus on slowing down and breathing from your stomach, not your chest.

Deep breathing will help to relax you when you are stressed.

TIP: Sleep with the window open and you will get a better nights sleep.

TIP: Take 10 deep stomach breaths when you get up in the morning to oxygenate your blood!

Rest

"Avoid any media or un-natural stimulation 45 minutes before you go to bed as this is what will play out in your sub-conscious mind as you sleep."

Sleep deeply with 8 hours of rest per night!

Most people generally need 8 hours sleep per night. If you are not waking feeling refreshed and rested you need to get to bed earlier.

A consistent sleep pattern is good for the body. Go to bed and get up at the same time each night.

TIP: Some experts say the hours before midnight are worth double for sleep. Get to bed earlier if you can.

Trust

Live in peace with a life full of great relationships!

This is all about the mental and spiritual side of health.

Make sure that you go to bed each night free from stress and worry. If not, deal with the issues.

If you are harboring any grudges or are not at peace with anyone, make things right and forgive without hesitation.

Keep fully focused and on track with your long term goals.

TIP: Search out and find the wonderful things that your creator God can do in your life.

TIP: Surprise a family member or friend with a visit, gift or words of encouragement to brighten their day.

"In everything, do to others what you would have them do to you." Matthew 7:12

Salads are really fun to make. Just choose some great fresh ingredients, pile them in a big mixing bowl, add lots of interesting colours, shapes and flavours and you have a great salad. They are really meals in themselves. Here is a selection of some of our favourite salads at Revive and some that are easy to make at home.

Salads

This salad was discovered due to shortage of our normal lettuce. One day in our first few months our normal lettuce was not able to be delivered. My chef at the time threw some ingredients together with another lettuce that was available and it became one of the most popular salads at Revive. We only have it during the summer months as that is when most lettuce is freshest and most plentiful.

Cos Caesar

MAKES 8 X 1 CUP SERVES

3 slices thick wholemeal bread

2 tablespoons rice bran oil

½ teaspoon salt

1 medium cos (romaine) lettuce

100g (3oz) feta cheese

¼ cup garlic aioli (page 150)

1. Cut the bread into cubes, mix with oil and salt. Roast at 180°C (350°F) for around 20 - 30 minutes or until just crisp.

2. Slice the lettuce into 2cm (1in) strips. Wash in cold water and dry in a lettuce spinner or between some paper towels.

3. Cut feta cheese into 1cm (½in) chunks.

4. Place all ingredients (except dressing) into a bowl and mix.

5. Put on plate or platter and drizzle garlic aioli over the top.

If the lettuce is clean, crisp and fresh you may not need to wash it.

Optional: you can add hard boiled eggs to this salad.

Cos (Romaine) Lettuce

Cos is a crunchy lettuce, and in my opinion, is the best lettuce around. It is also known as romaine lettuce. You can use this lettuce in any salad that requires normal lettuce.

Probably our most popular salad at Revive. I try to take it off the menu occasionally so people do not get too tired of it. However I get regular e-mails asking when it will be back. Hence we have it in our salad bar about 95% of the time.

Moroccan Chickpeas

MAKES 5 X 1 CUP SERVES

1 large carrot

1 cup green beans (fresh or frozen)

2 x 400g (12oz) cans chickpeas (garbanzo beans) drained

¼ cup sultanas

¼ cup diced dates

¼ cup garlic aioli (page 150)

1 teaspoon ground cumin

1 teaspoon ground turmeric

½ teaspoon salt

¼ cup parsley

2 tablespoons sweet chilli sauce

½ cup date puree (page 154) or 2 tablespoons honey

1. Grate carrot.

2. Cut green beans into 5cm (2in) lengths with diagonal cuts. Bring a pot of water to the boil and cook for 2 minutes.

3. Assemble all ingredients in a bowl and mix well.

Cook your own fresh chickpeas for this recipe. They are amazing!

Chickpeas (Garbanzo Beans)

My favourite legume. They are smooth, soft and go with many different flavours. They are also high in protein. Always keep them canned in your cupboard, or cook your own and store in the freezer for quick use.

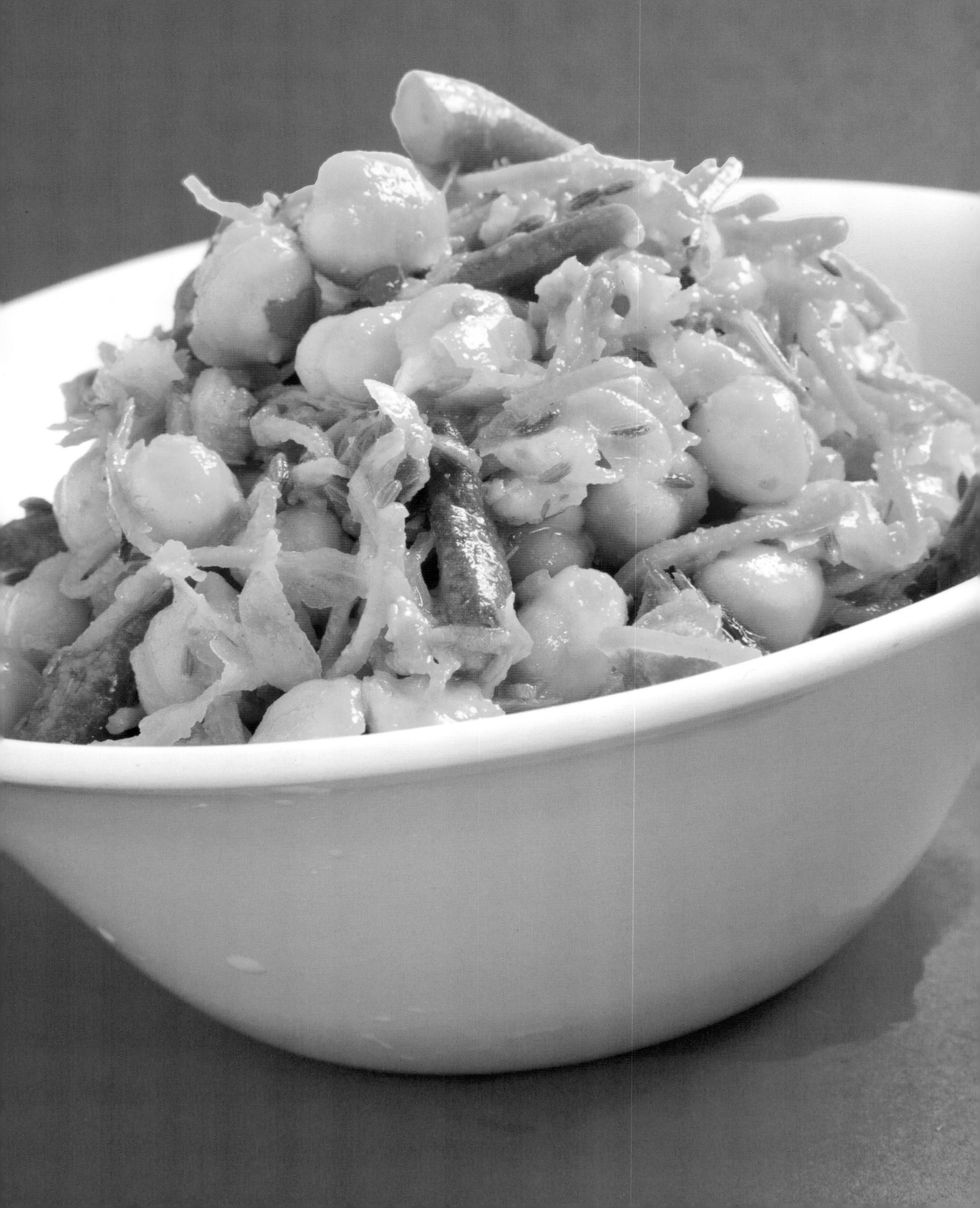

It is always nice to add a little crunch to a salad. Seeds are full of nutrients and transform a classic coleslaw into something special. They also add colour and quality protein at the same time.

Seedy Slaw

MAKES 6 X 1 CUP SERVES

2 cups finely sliced red cabbage

2 cups finely sliced white cabbage

2 cups grated carrot

¾ cup mixed seeds
  - pumpkin seeds
  - black sesame seeds
  - white sesame seeds
  - sunflower seeds
  - poppy seeds

¼ cup chopped parsley

LEMON DRESSING:

¼ cup rice bran oil

1 clove garlic crushed

½ teaspoon ground cumin

½ teaspoon salt

2 tablespoons lemon juice

1. Cut/grate by hand, or use a food processor with a grating / slicing blade to prepare vegetables.

2. Make lemon dressing with stick blender, blender or shaker.

3. Mix all ingredients together in a big mixing bowl.

Grated beetroot is a great addition to this salad if you want to add some extra colour and an earthy flavour.

This salad will not keep so eat it the same day it is made. If you want to prepare - grate/slice the vegetables the day before. You can then mix in the dressing and seeds just before serving.

Pumpkin Seeds

A favourite seed of mine. Is not only a great flavour in salads or meals, but is a useful green garnish ingredient that can transform a dish.

An all-time classic favourite. We only have this at Revive in the warmer months when the ingredients are plentiful, good quality and cost effective. Make sure you use kalamata olives as these are the best! We are unique in that we use fresh spinach in our Greek Salad as it just seems to work well.

Classic Greek Salad

MAKES 8 X 1 CUP SERVES

4 large tomatoes

1 medium cucumber

½ small red onion

100g (3oz) feta cheese crumbled

½ cup pitted kalamata olives

3 cups baby spinach or ripped large spinach

2 tablespoons lemon juice (freshly squeezed)

1 tablespoon olive oil

1. Cut tomatoes, cucumber and onion into 2cm (1in) cubes.

2. Put all ingredients (except feta) into a mixing bowl and combine together gently.

3. Add feta last and give a quick mix.

Keep your tomatoes at room temperature, not in the refrigerator as they will keep more flavour.

You can serve this dish without the dressing.

Kalamata Olives

Olives give a great flavour to many dishes. Kalamata olives are the best ones to get as they have great flavour. I prefer pitted olives as they are quicker to use and there are no issues with olive stones breaking your teeth!

An amazing salad that is always popular. Best in winter when these vegetables are plentiful. Be warned this is a high prep salad with lots of cutting and roasting. But the results are worth it. It is lovely served warm or cold.

Sweet Chilli Roast Veges

MAKES 8 X 1 CUP SERVES

10 cups raw diced vegetables of your choice:
- kumara (sweet potato)
- pumpkin
- carrot
- beetroot
- potato
- red capsicum (bell pepper)
- courgette (zucchini)
- red onion

4 tablespoons rice bran oil

¼ cup parsley chopped for garnish

DRESSING:

2 tablespoons rice bran oil

4 tablespoons sweet chilli sauce

1 tablespoon cider vinegar

2 tablespoons whole grain mustard

1 teaspoon salt

3 tablespoons water

1. Dice vegetables in different shapes but keep overall size around 4cm (1½in).

2. Roast vegetables with oil for about 30 minutes. When soft (but not mushy) put directly on your serving platter.

3. If you use beetroot it will need to cook separately for over 40 minutes and gently place on the top of other vegetables so it does not colour everything red.

4. Heat a small pan. Add dressing ingredients and stir until bubbling. Add more water if needed to get a ketchup-like texture.

5. Pour directly over roast vegetables.

6. Garnish with freshly chopped parsley and serve.

Make sure you get a good range of colours in your roast vege salad.

This salad will keep in the fridge for a couple of days and actually improves with a little time. However I will be very surprised if you end up with leftovers.

Sweet Chilli Sauce

Often called the chef's cheat sauce. This is a great sauce to add to a dish that needs something else. Most varieties are quite mild and not too hot. Many brands contain flavour enhancers so avoid these.

Another of the most requested salads at Revive and a unique way to serve Risotto. It is not truly a risotto as it does not have cream and parmesan cheese, but it is a favourite so it must work!

Mushroom Risotto Salad

MAKES 5 X 1 CUP SERVES

1 cup long grain
brown rice

2 cups boiling water

1 tablespoon rice bran oil

200g (6oz) button
mushrooms

½ cup garlic aioli
(page 150)

1 teaspoon dried thyme

1 teaspoon salt

2 tablespoons sweet
chilli sauce

½ cup frozen peas

¼ cup roasted peanuts

¼ cup chopped parsley
to garnish

1. Cook rice in water for 30 minutes (or use 3 cups pre-cooked rice).

2. Slice mushrooms thinly and cook in pot with oil for around 10 minutes until wilted. Drain liquid.

3. Mix all ingredients together in a bowl.

4. Garnish with parsley.

It is handy using dried herbs as they are in your pantry however always use fresh if you have them.

Long Grain Brown Rice

Do not settle for white rice. It is a poor quality grain with the goodness extracted.   Brown rice has more fibre and nutrients. When it is cooked properly it tastes great. And it only takes 30-35 minutes to cook on the stove top. I prefer long grain as it cooks faster and is softer to eat.

When beetroot is scarce and we take this off the menu I get a lot of requests to put it back on. People also tell me they travel out of their way to get this salad. Who would have thought a lentil salad could be so popular?

Balsamic Lentil & Roasted Beetroot Salad

MAKES 6 X 1 CUP SERVES

1 cup dry french green (puy) lentils

3 cups boiling water

2 large beetroot

1 red capsicum (bell pepper) diced

1 green capsicum (bell pepper) diced

½ teaspoon salt

2 tablespoons sweet chilli sauce

¼ cup chopped parsley for garnish

BALSAMIC DRESSING:

1 tablespoon balsamic vinegar

1 teaspoon cider vinegar

2 cloves garlic

1 teaspoon whole grain mustard

2 teaspoons honey or date puree

¼ cup oil

1. Combine lentils and water in a pot (lid on). Bring to the boil and simmer (just boiling) for 30 minutes or until just soft.

2. Ensure you drain your lentils well to avoid a runny sauce in the bottom.

3. Cut the ends and any hard bits off the beetroot and dice into 2cm (1 in) chunks. Put on an oven tray and mix with the oil.

4. Bake for 40 minutes at 180°C (350°F) or until soft.

5. Make the dressing with a stick blender or a shaker container.

6. Combine all ingredients in a mixing bowl.

7. Serve with parsley or other green garnish.

Beetroot

This colourful vegetable can transform the colour and look of a meal. Handy tinned, or buy it raw and grate or slice it. It is amazing roasted!

This is the substitute salad for the Moroccan Chickpea salad. We cannot have a salad on all the time so I occasionally pop this on on the salad menu to give the Moroccan one a break. While not as popular it is a really nice salad.

Italian Chickpeas

MAKES 4 X 1 CUP SERVES

10 sun-dried tomatoes

½ cup kalamata olives pitted

½ green capsicum (bell pepper)

½ red capsicum (bell pepper)

2 x 400g (12oz) cans of chickpeas (garbanzo beans)

ITALIAN DRESSING:

1 tablespoon date puree or honey

½ teaspoon salt

1 tablespoon lemon juice

1 tablespoon balsamic vinegar

¼ cup oil

1. Soak sun-dried tomatoes in some boiling water for around 10 minutes. Drain and slice thinly.

2. Chop vegetables and olives into small cubes.

3. Put dressing ingredients in a blender or food processor and blend. Alternatively you can shake vigorously in a closed jar.

4. Combine all ingredients in a big bowl and mix.

5. Serve with parsley to garnish.

This salad would be great stuffed inside fresh wholemeal pita bread with some lettuce and avocado.

Sun Dried Tomatoes

These little bursts of flavour are great in salads and meals. The best way to buy them is dried, and then soak them yourself. You can also buy them in oil but they are usually fairly expensive that way.

In 2009 Revive was a finalist in the "Great New Zealand Potato Challenge" with this salad. It also gets the most "oohs and ahhs" in my cooking demonstrations as something unique. You can make the dukkah very inexpensively or you can buy it pre-mixed in most gourmet stores.

Dukkah Roasted Potatoes

MAKES 5 X 1 CUP SERVES

3 large white
washed potatoes

1 tablespoon rice bran oil

¼ cup garlic aioli
(page 150)

½ cup dukkah mix
(page 149)

½ teaspoon salt

¼ cup raw or roasted
cashew nuts

2 tablespoons finely
chopped parsley

1 teaspoon ground cumin

1. Cut potatoes into 2cm (1in) cubes.

2. Roast potatoes coated in oil at 180°C (350°F) degrees for 30 minutes until soft.

3. Let them cool so they do not go mushy when mixing.

4. Mix all ingredients together in a bowl.

5. Serve warm or chilled.

Have aioli and dukkah ready in the refrigerator made up in bulk so you can use it in this or similar recipes any time with little fuss.

Potatoes (Spuds)

Traditionally an Irish staple - potatoes are great carbohydrates and good for bulking up food. They are great roasted with a little oil. I prefer to buy pre washed potatoes and use without peeling.

I love bean salads and this is our most popular one. Combining all the lovely colours results in an amazing salad. You can use any combination of beans and chickpeas. This recipe is very flexible.

Sweet Bean Medley

MAKES 8 X 1 CUP SERVES

1 red capsicum (bell pepper)

400g (12oz) can red kidney beans drained

400g (12oz) can chickpeas (garbanzo beans) drained

400g (12oz) can white beans drained

1½ cups frozen corn or 400g (12oz) can sweet corn drained

1½ cups green beans (frozen or fresh) diagonally sliced

1 teaspoon salt

BALSAMIC DRESSING:

1 tablespoon balsamic vinegar

1 teaspoon cider vinegar

2 cloves garlic

1 teaspoon whole grain mustard

2 teaspoons honey or date puree

¼ cup oil

1. Mix dressing in a blender/food processor or with a stick blender. Add all ingredients (except oil) and blend, then add the oil and blend.

2. Chop capsicum finely and put in a mixing bowl.

3. Steam or boil green beans for around 4 minutes to lightly cook. They should remain green and solid. Add to bowl.

4. Add canned beans and remaining ingredients and mix.

5. Taste for saltiness and sweetness and adjust if necessary.

You can also make the dressing by shaking all ingredients in a glass jar or specially designed dressing shaker.

Green Beans

These make excellent ingredients for salads as they give great crunch and nice colour. They do need to be steamed before using although only lightly as you want them to stay firm. They are also available frozen and are great to have in the freezer all year round.

My favourite Thai salad. I accidentally ordered too much green curry paste and needed to use it up so tried it with some seasonal vegetables one spring and came up with this creation. Green curry paste is usually hotter so do not use too much!

Thai Green Curry Veges

MAKES 6 X 1 CUP SERVES

2 large kumara
(sweet potato)

2 tablespoons rice bran oil

½ teaspoon salt

1 head broccoli

1 red capsicum (bell pepper)

100g (3oz) can bamboo shoots

¼ head cauliflower

¼ cup aioli (page 150)

1 teaspoon Thai green curry paste

¼ cup warm water

2 tablespoons honey or date puree

1. Cut kumara into 2cm (1in) cubes and mix with oil spread on an oven tray.

2. Roast for 15 minutes at 180°C (250°F) or until soft.

3. Cut broccoli and cauliflower into florets and steam for 2 minutes. Do not overcook.

4. Cut capsicum into small cubes.

5. Mix water, honey and curry paste together to form a runny paste.

6. Combine all ingredients in a mixing bowl.

If you do not like things hot, start with just a little curry paste. It is easier to add more later than to take it out. A little bit goes a long way.

Bamboo Shoots

Best purchased in little cans these give any Thai dish an authentic flavour and texture. They are quite bland so do need a strong flavour to go with.

This is a salad I enjoy making at home. It is so quick and colourful.

Corn & Pepper Fiesta

MAKES 4 X 1 CUP SERVES

2 x 400g (12oz) cans whole kernel corn drained

1 red capsicum (bell pepper)

3 spring onions (scallions)

2 tablespoons lemon juice

1 tablespoon olive oil

¼ teaspoon salt

1. Finely chop the spring onions and capsicum.

2. Combine all ingredients in a mixing bowl.

You can also use frozen corn for this recipe. Simply run it under hot water for about 30 seconds to defrost it. You do not need to cook it.

Spring Onions (Scallions)

Colour, freshness and crunch. These are great in most salads. Just chop them up and sprinkle on top. Great with any Asian food like noodles, or tofu. Make sure you use the whole vegetable.

I am a big fan of long grain brown rice as it only takes around 30 minutes to cook. It is also softer and more like white rice which makes it easier for people to transition to brown rice (we do not serve white rice at Revive). I wanted a different rice salad so I created this one with short grain brown rice and it was an instant hit! I also find that anything with curry or peanuts always sells well.

Chewy Indonesian Rice

MAKES 3 X 1 CUP SERVES

1 cup short grain brown rice

2 cups boiling water

1 spring onion (scallion)

1 red capsicum (bell pepper)

1 green capsicum (bell pepper)

¼ cup currants

¼ cup roasted peanuts

½ teaspoon crushed chilli or pinch chilli flakes

½ teaspoon salt

1 teaspoon curry ground

2 tablespoons date puree or honey

LEMON DRESSING:

¼ cup rice bran oil

1 clove garlic chopped or crushed

½ teaspoon ground cumin

½ teaspoon salt

2 tablespoons lemon juice

1. Cook the rice with the boiling water (lid on) for around 40 minutes or until cooked and sticky.

2. Chop the spring onions and capsicum finely.

3. Combine the lemon dressing ingredients in a blender and blend (or use a stick blender).

4. Combine all ingredients well in a big mixing bowl.

If you pre-cook your rice and it sticks together or does not look that appealing, try rinsing it in some boiling water to freshen it up.

Curry Powder

Curry powder is just a blend of various spices such as ground turmeric, coriander, cumin, fenugreek, chilli and others. It is great for a quick general curry taste. I generally go for the mild varieties as it is the flavour I am after, not the heat.

Noodles are boring by nature but they soak up strong flavours very well. This is Revive's most popular noodle salad.

Thai Satay Kumara Noodles

MAKES 6 X 1 CUP SERVES

2 large kumara
(sweet potato)

2 tablespoons rice bran oil

100g (3oz) long Rice
Noodles 3mm ($^{1}/_{10}$in)

2 cups satay sauce
(page 152)

1 red capsicum
(bell pepper)

2 spring onions (scallions)

½ teaspoon salt

2 tablespoons sweet
chilli sauce

1. Cut kumara into 2cm (1in) cubes, combine with oil and roast for around 15 minutes at 180°C (350°F).

2. Bring a large pot of water to the boil, add the rice noodles and simmer for 8 minutes (or until noodles are just soft).

3. Drain immediately and rinse with cold water to prevent them from over cooking. Drain again in sieve or colander.

4. Chop the spring onions and capsicum.

5. Combine all ingredients together.

Add extra satay sauce if you are not going to serve this salad straight away. The noodles will suck up the liquid and make them dry.

Rice Noodles

Rice noodles make a great base for salads. They come in various sizes but our favourite is the 3mm size ($^{1}/_{10}$ inch). They are also a great gluten free option. Available from any Asian store and some regular supermarkets..

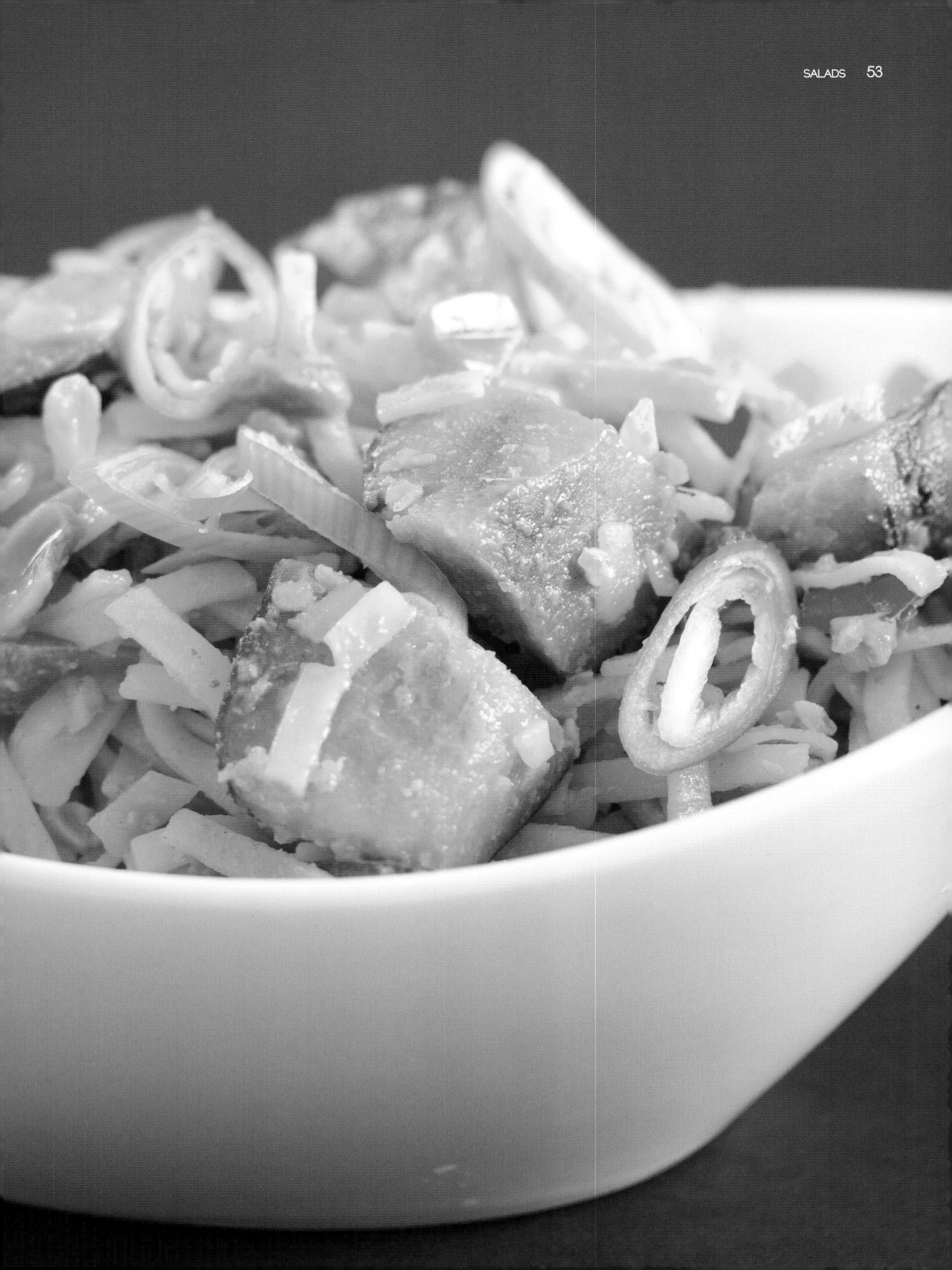

Put "Honey Mustard" on any dish in a cafe and it will sell well. It is one of those flavour combinations that everyone loves.

Honey Mustard Roasted Potatoes

MAKES 6 X 1 CUP SERVES

1.5kg (3lb) white potatoes washed (around 3-4 large)

4 tablespoons rice bran oil

1 teaspoon salt

4 tablespoons liquid honey

¼ cup chopped parsley

2 tablespoons whole grain mustard

1. Chop potatoes (unpeeled) into 2cm (1in) cubes and mix with oil in a roasting tray.

2. Bake at 180°C (350°F) for around 40 minutes or until soft.

3. Let potatoes cool down a little or they can get mushy when mixing.

4. Mix with all other ingredients in a mixing bowl.

This salad is lovely served warm.

You can also mix in some baby spinach to this salad just before serving if you need more green happening on your table.

Whole Grain Mustard

A nice flavour to add to many dishes for a little extra zing. Nice with potatoes in salads, and some dressings. Check that there are no flavour enhancers in the brand you buy.

My favourite rice salad. It is great in the middle of winter when leeks are plentiful. The secret however is the Chermoula dressing which is infused with lots of delicious Moroccan spices.

Moroccan Leek Rice

MAKES 6 X 1 CUP SERVES

1 cup long grain brown rice

2 cups boiling water

1 large leek

2 tablespoons rice bran oil

¼ cup chermoula dressing (page 151)

¼ cup parsley

1 red capsicum (bell pepper) sliced

½ teaspoon salt

1. Cook rice in water for 30 minutes with the lid on.

2. Slice the leeks thinly and roast with the oil for 10 minutes at 180°C (350°F) or until soft. Alternatively you could cook in a pan or pot on the stove.

3. Combine all ingredients in a bowl and mix.

4. Check saltiness and flavour and adjust if necessary.

Cook extra rice and keep it in the refrigerator so you can easily make another rice meal or salad in minutes.

Leeks

Leeks are a great winter vegetable and awesome in soups, salads and virtually any meal. They are exceptional when sliced and roasted with a little oil. Roasting makes them sweeter.

This juicy salad was originally called a 4C salad (carrots, cashews, coriander and coconut). However there was a world shortage of cashews in 2011 resulting in very high prices. I had to replace them with almonds. I changed the name of the salads as "3CA" does not have a good ring to it. But the almond version is equally as good.

Almond Carrot Crunch

MAKES 4 X 1 CUP SERVES

4 large carrots

½ cup raw almonds

¼ cup roughly chopped coriander

1 teaspoon ground coriander

2 tablespoons honey or date puree

½ teaspoon salt

optional: ¼ cup shredded coconut

LEMON DRESSING:

¼ cup rice bran oil

1 clove garlic crushed

½ teaspoon ground cumin

½ teaspoon salt

2 tablespoons lemon juice

1. Grate the carrots by hand or in your food processor. If they are fresh and clean you do not need to peel them.

2. Make dressing with stick blender or shaker.

3. Chop the almonds roughly or you can use slivered almonds.

4. Combine all ingredients.

Optional: add some shredded coconut as a garnish.

Optional: dry roast the almonds in the oven for around 8 minutes at 180°C (350°F) for a greater flavour.

Grated Carrot

This is an excellent ingredient to add to many dishes and salads. It adds moisture, colour, flavour and freshness. You can use a hand grater or the attachments for your food processor that are probably gathering dust in the back of your cupboard. Make sure you try out the julienne blade too.

For those who do not like cauliflower, you have to try this salad. Satay sauce plus peanuts equals lots of flavour that is irresistible!

Satay Cauliflower with Peanuts

MAKES 6 X 1 CUP SERVES

½ head medium
sized cauliflower

2 cups satay sauce (page 152)

½ cup roasted peanuts

1 cup mung bean sprouts

fresh coriander (cilantro)
for garnish

1. Chop cauliflower into small florets. Cut up the stalk too. Do not waste it.

2. Boil cauliflower for around 5 minutes until just soft.

3. Combine all ingredients.

Keep a close eye on the cauliflower while it is cooking. Too hard and it will taste raw. Too soft and it will be mushy and tasteless. The key is to get it just cooked but still firm.

Cauliflower

A nice crunchy vegetable that can go great in many dishes including stir fries. For something different try roasting cauliflower whole and serving with satay sauce. Or blend into a soup or casserole for a creamy texture.

When new vegetables come in season and there is no specific salad to put them in I create a mingle salad like this one. Simply combining vegetables and a great dressing is how many of our most popular salads have been created!

Spring Kumara Mingle

MAKES 6 x 1 CUP SERVES

2 large red kumara
(sweet potato)

1 tablespoon rice bran oil

400g (12oz) can red kidney beans (or freshly cooked)

¼ cup chermoula dressing (page 151)

4 cups fresh spinach roughly torn

½ teaspoon salt

1. Wash the kumara and chop into 2cm (1in) cubes leaving the skin on.

2. Toss with oil on an oven tray. Bake at 180°C (350°F) for around 15 minutes or until soft.

3. Mix all ingredients in a bowl.

Do not peel the kumara unless it is old and has a tough skin. It will be fine when roasted and you do not want to throw away all that colour and goodness.

Kumara (Sweet Potato)

A great sweet vegetable that goes with almost anything. Best roasted with a little oil and salt. When chopped they take around 15 minutes to roast. The most common colours are red, gold and orange. Try them all, they all have their unique flavours. Just do not over-cook them as they go mushy easily.

I love the freshness of this salad. It is one of our staple salads in the winter. I was searching for an ingredient to add to our mesclun salad and had just purchased a new julienne blade for our food processor. My kitchen hand was peeling pumpkin at the time, so I threw it through the processor to test it out, thinking it would probably jam up. However it produced these lovely colourful strands of pumpkin that work amazingly with this salad.

Tuscan Mesclun

MAKES 8 X 1 CUP SERVES

100g (3oz) bag mesclun lettuce

100g (3oz) feta cheese crumbled

½ cup raw or roasted cashew nuts

2 cups grated or julienne pumpkin (raw) - this is around 1/4 of a medium pumpkin

OPTIONAL INGREDIENTS:

½ cup sun dried tomatoes cut into strips

¼ cup kalamata olives

1 red pepper julienned

1.   Lightly toss all ingredients together and serve.

2.   Add optional ingredients if you wish. This salad is very versatile.

Use your julienne attachment on your food processer. It is really quick to make vegetables look awesome, and much faster than chopping by hand.

When storing lettuce salads in the fridge put a wet tea towel over the top. This will prevent the lettuce from drying out while still allowing it to breathe.

Mesclun Lettuce

This is usually hydroponically grown and hence available all year round. It is great in winter when the usual lettuce varieties are bad quality. Mesclun contains a blend of different leaves, fresh and some are bitter. Often rinsing in cold water can bring some slightly wilted mesclun back to life.

In the middle of one winter when green produce was scarce, of low quality and expensive, I was searching for a fresh winter salad. So I took the traditional waldorf salad and "revived" it.

Revive-dorf Salad

MAKES 6 X 1 CUP SERVES

3 large red apples

2 big stalks celery

½ cup garlic aioli
(page 150)

50g (1½oz) (about 2 cups)
baby spinach

1 tablespoon lemon juice

optional: ¼ cup walnuts

1. Core and chop apples into 2cm (1in) cubes.

2. Slice celery into 1cm (½in) pieces.

3. Mix all ingredients in a bowl.

The apple will oxidise (go brown) quickly so you need to prepare this salad close to serving time. Ensure you dress the apples quickly as this will help them stop going brown.

Celery

A great fresh vegetable that adds crunch to any salad. Do not be scared to use the leafy part as well. Celery is also great chopped up and used in soups and casseroles.

This colourful salad is inspired by Pacific Island ingredients like coconut and lime juice.

Pacifika Coleslaw

MAKES 8 X 1 CUP SERVES

3 cups sliced
purple cabbage

3 cups grated carrot

2 tablespoons finely
chopped parsley

2 tablespoons date puree
or honey

2 tablespoons grated/
shredded coconut

4 tablespoons lime juice

LEMON DRESSING:

¼ cup rice bran oil

1 clove garlic crushed

½ teaspoon ground cumin

½ teaspoon salt

2 tablespoons lemon juice

1. Grate carrot and slice cabbage as per ingredient directions.

2. Make dressing with stick blender, blender or shaker.

3. Combine all ingredients in a bowl and mix well.

Purple Cabbage

This is my favourite cabbage. It adds so much colour to a cabbage dish. It can be used anywhere cabbage is used and is especially great in stir fries.

Hotpots are a dish we serve that contains a sauce, a protein and are served over brown rice. They could be a curry, stew, casserole or any similar dish. The beauty about making them is that you just keep firing ingredients into a big pot and you have a healthy delicious meal!

Hotpots & Stir Fries

This dish was on the menu in the first few weeks we started Revive. It was in the days when we had a static menu - we now have a menu that changes every day but we regularly feature this dish. You can make it thick or runny depending on how you like it. And you can add some chillis to spice it up if you are into hot food!

Pumpkin, Spinach, Ginger & Tofu Curry

MAKES 8 X 1 CUP SERVES

1 large chopped onion

3 tablespoons ginger puree

2 cloves garlic chopped or crushed

2 tablespoons oil

1 tablespoon ground cumin

1 tablespoon ground turmeric

1 tablespoon ground coriander

3 tablespoons honey or date puree

1 cup water

2 x 400g (12oz) cans chopped tomatoes

200ml (6fl oz) coconut cream

2 teaspoons salt

2 cups diced roasted pumpkin cubes

2 cups frozen spinach

600g (19oz) pack tofu firm cubed 1cm (½in)

1. Saute onion, garlic, oil, ginger until clear and well cooked.

2. Add spices and salt and mix well.

3. Blend tomatoes with a stick blender and add with water to the pot and bring back to the boil.

4. Add coconut cream, honey and salt and stir.

5. Mix in all remaining ingredients carefully so as not to damage.

6. Serve on brown rice or rice noodles with optional chilli garnish.

Ginger

Ginger is a great natural flavour-enhancing ingredient. Most of the time you do not know it is in a dish but it just adds a depth of flavour. Ginger is great for digestion. You can chop finely or make your own ginger puree by blending with some oil and storing in the fridge.

Butter Chicken is the biggest selling dish in Indian restaurants by a country mile. So I created this dish in 2010 that does not have chicken (of course), cream or that red food colouring that is normally in the traditional dish. It quickly became a Revive favourite.

Not Butter Chicken

MAKES 8 X 1 CUP SERVES

600g (20oz) pack firm tofu

3 large carrots

1 large onion diced

2 cloves garlic chopped or crushed

2 tablespoons oil

1 tablespoon ginger puree

1 teaspoon ground cumin

1 teaspoon ground turmeric

1 teaspoon ground coriander

1 teaspoon garam masala powder

1/8 teaspoon chilli powder

1 teaspoon salt or to taste

2 x 400g (12oz) cans tomatoes blended

200ml (6fl oz) coconut cream

1. Ahead of time take your tofu, drain it, and store in your freezer for at least 2 days. It will change into a nice chicken-like texture. Defrost and slice into 2cm (1in) strips.

2. Slice the carrots thinly and roast with a little oil for 20 minutes at 150°C (300°F).

3. Saute onions, ginger, garlic and oil in large pot until clear.

4. Add spices and mix well.

5. Add tomatoes and cook for around 5 minutes or until bubbling.

6. Gently mix in the remaining ingredients.

7. Check heat and salt for your taste and add more salt/chilli as required.

8. Serve on brown rice.

Always have some frozen tofu in your freezer so you can whip up this meal in a very short time.

Tofu

A bland and boring looking ingredient. However add some great flavour and mix with some good ingredients and it makes a wholesome and delicious meal. You can pre-freeze it and it will develop a texture similar to chicken.

This dish is usually a soup, but we make it thick, add chickpeas and serve on rice to make it a hotpot. A meal in itself. We get a lot of comments from people who think it should be a soup. However compared to other food naming liberties I take, it is probably one of the lesser food crimes I have committed at Revive.

Corn & Potato Chowder

MAKES 6 X 1 CUP SERVES

1 large sliced onion

1 tablespoon rice bran oil

4 cloves garlic chopped or crushed

1 teaspoon crushed chilli (optional)

1 teaspoon dried thyme

3 cups boiling water

1 large unpeeled potato cut into 2cm (1in) squares

1 large unpeeled kumara (sweet potato) cut into 2cm (1in) squares

2 cups frozen or canned corn

1 stalk celery sliced 1cm (½in) (include leaves)

1 large red onion

2 tablespoons honey

1 large red capsicum (bell pepper) diced

400g (12oz) can chickpeas (garbanzo beans)

100ml (3fl oz) coconut cream

1 teaspoon salt

1. Saute oil, onion, chilli, garlic and thyme until clear.

2. Add water, kumara and potato and cook for around 20 minutes or until soft.

3. With a potato masher mash most of the mix so it thickens, but still retains chunky bits.

4. Add celery and corn and cook for approximately 5 minutes.

5. In a small frying pan, saute the red onion and honey for around 10 minutes. Add to pot.

6. Add remaining ingredients and bring back to the boil.

Delicious served with some hummus or pesto on top.

Sweet Corn

Adds amazing colour and flavour to many dishes. Have a bag in your freezer or canned in your pantry. Do not combine with frozen peas/carrots or your food will look like school cafeteria meals.

Satays are always popular at Revive - especially in the winter. We make this dish with either chickpeas or tofu. Both go well in this recipe.

Indonesian Chickpea Satay

MAKES 8 X 1 CUP SERVES

2 large carrots

1 large chopped onion

2 tablespoons oil

2 cloves garlic chopped or crushed

3 tablespoons ginger puree

1 pinch cayenne pepper

1 teaspoon ground turmeric

1 teaspoon ground cumin

½ cup peanut butter

½ cup hot water

2 x 400ml (12fl oz) cans tomatoes (blended)

200ml/6fl oz coconut cream

2 x 400g (12oz) cans chickpeas (garbanzo beans)

1 teaspoon salt

3 tablespoons date puree or honey

1. Slice and roast carrots for around 20 minutes at 180°C (350°F).

2. In a large pot or pan cook onion, garlic, oil and ginger until clear.

3. Stir in spices.

4. Mix peanut butter and hot water to make a pourable paste and add to the pot.

5. Add tomatoes and heat until boiling.

6. Add salt and coconut cream and date puree.

7. Add chickpeas and carrots.

Optional: garnish with freshly chopped chives or other fresh herbs.

Peanut Butter

Peanut butter can add a great nutty flavour to many dishes. Often it is easier to mix with a little water to thin it down before adding to the main dish. Use sparingly as it is high in fat. Also buy natural where you can, as some brands are full of preservatives and sugar.

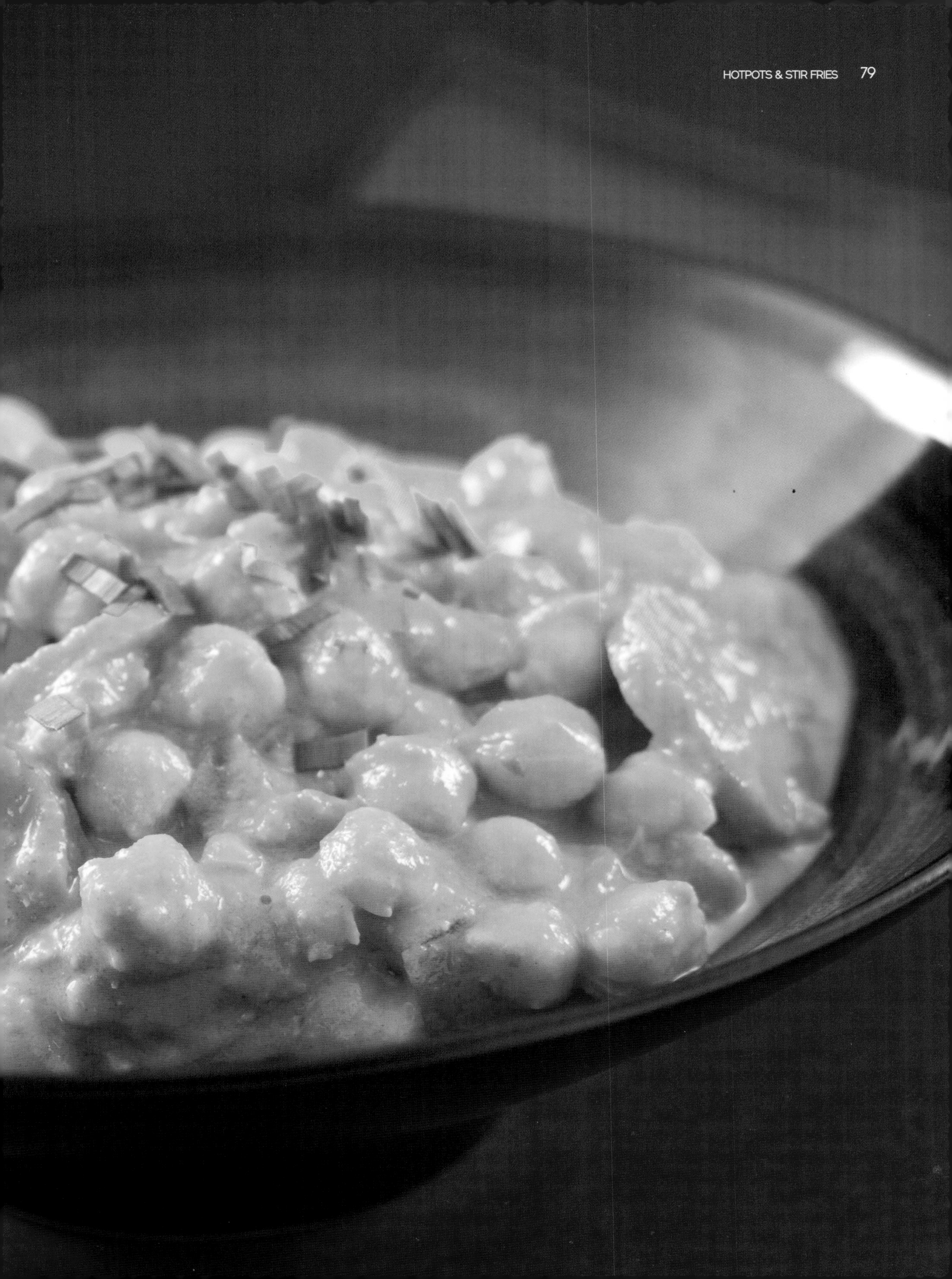

Thai food is very flavoursome. Here you can make a Thai curry with all of the fragrant ingredients. While you may not get a curry the same as a traditional Thai chef, you can get a delicious, tasty meal that is pretty close.

Thai Red Curry with Tofu

MAKES 5 X 1 CUP SERVES

1 medium onion chopped in half and finely sliced

2 tablespoons rice bran oil

2 tablespoons ginger or ginger puree

1 tablespoon red curry paste

½ cup hot water

2 tablespoons lemongrass finely chopped

2 tablespoons honey (or date puree)

1 teaspoon salt

400g (12oz) can tomatoes blended

200g (6oz) can bamboo shoots - drained

10 kaffir lime leaves (optional)

1 teaspoon ground coriander

½ red capsicum (bell pepper) sliced finely

½ green capsicum (bell pepper) sliced finely

600g (19oz) firm tofu diced into 1cm (½ in) cubes

400ml (12fl oz) coconut cream

1. In a large pot saute onion, oil and ginger until soft.

2. Mix the curry paste with hot water and add.

3. Add all other ingredients (except tofu and coconut cream) and cook for around 5 minutes until bubbling.

4. Add tofu and coconut cream and stir in gently for a couple of minutes until heated.

5. Garnish with fresh herbs.

The list of ingredients may seem daunting, however most of them are one-off purchases. Once they are in your fridge or pantry you can use them over again.

If you find some ingredients hard to source, it probably will not matter if you leave one or two out.

Kaffir Lime Leaves

These little leaves are the most fragrant items you can put in a dish. Kaffir Lime trees grow easily, like a lemon tree. You use the leaves in cooking by either finely chopping up and adding to a dish, or left in whole while cooking. They are also available frozen from many Asian stores.

After eating this dish at an Indian restaurant I knew we had to have a version of it on the menu at Revive. I keep reminding my customers that while it looks brown and scary, it does taste great. Once people brave the first sample, they agree and love it.

Dahl Makhani

MAKES 6 X 1 CUP SERVES

1 large onion diced

2 tablespoons oil

1 tablespoon chopped ginger or ginger puree

4 cloves garlic chopped or crushed

1 tablespoon crushed chilli or pinch chilli flakes

1 teaspoon garam masala

1 teaspoon cumin seeds

1 teaspoon ground turmeric

1 cup urid dahl (ideally split)

3 cups water

400g (12 oz) can chopped tomatoes

3 tablespoons honey (or date puree)

1½ teaspoon salt

200ml (6 fl oz) coconut cream

400g (12 oz) can red kidney beans drained

1. If urid dahl is whole, soak overnight in some water. Drain and rinse well before cooking.

2. In a pot, saute onions, garlic, ginger and oil until clear.

3. Add spices and chilli.

4. Add soaked dahl and water and cook for around 1 hour or until soft.

5. Add tomatoes and honey and blend all with a stick blender.

6. Add coconut cream, salt and kidney beans and serve garnished with fresh coriander.

Reserve some of the kidney beans for a garnish.

You will need to soak the urid dahl overnight if it is whole.

Urid Dahl

Urid Dahl has a unique and bland flavour by itself. But with many other flavours and ingredients it tastes great and is worthwhile having in your kitchen for those times when you want something different.

I love ratatouille, however as it is mostly a side dish, the traditional version does not contain any protein and cannot be used a meal in its own right . One day I had some leftover red lentils in the fridge and had just found two large and beautiful eggplants at my vege shop. I thought I would make a different ratatouille and this great dish was born. Some Mediterranean ingredients (eggplant, peppers & mushrooms) can be a little pricey in the winter so this is more of a spring/summer dish.

Dahl-a-touille

MAKES 8 X 1 CUP SERVES

1 cup dried red lentils

3 cups boiling water

1 onion finely chopped

1 eggplant (aubergine) diced into 1cm (½in) cubes

1 big stalk celery diced

2 cups mushrooms sliced

1 tablespoon ginger puree or chopped ginger

4 cloves garlic finely chopped or crushed

2 teaspoons salt

2 tablespoons oil

2 tablespoons honey or date puree

400g(12oz) can tomatoes chopped

1 small green capsicum (bell pepper) finely diced

1 cup frozen peas

1. Cook lentils and boiling water in their own pot for around 12 minutes or until soft.

2. In a large pot or frying pan, saute the onion, oil, garlic, ginger, celery, eggplant and mushrooms until they are soft.

3. Combine all the other ingredients, stir and bring to the boil. Turn down the heat and simmer for around 5 minutes to let the flavours mingle.

Make sure the eggplant is nice and soft before adding the lentils. You do not want uncooked eggplant.

Eggplant (Aubergine)

A delicious Mediterranean vegetable that is amazing when roasted or lightly pan fried. You can roast in the oven it but needs lots of oil and salt. I prefer just pan frying with other vegetables if possible.

This is a nice variation of a traditional Indian dish with white beans and potato. It also uses cashew nuts as a cream to give it smoothness and thickness.

Malai Kofta

MAKES 8 X 1 CUP SERVINGS

2 large potatoes

1 onion sliced

2 cloves garlic finely chopped or crushed

2 teaspoons finely chopped ginger or ginger puree

½ teaspoon nutmeg

1 teaspoon ground turmeric

¼ teaspoon clove powder

1 teaspoon ground coriander

⅛ teaspoon chilli powder

1 teaspoon salt

2 x 400g (12oz) cans tomatoes blended

1 cup cashew nuts

1 cup water

2 tablespoons honey or date puree

2 tablespoons oil

1 tablespoon poppy seeds

2 cans white beans drained

1. Chop potatoes into 2cm (1in) cubes and roast with a little oil for around 30 minutes at 180°C (350°F) or until soft.

2. In a large pot saute onions, garlic, ginger and oil until clear.

3. Add spices and salt and mix well.

4. Add tomatoes and cook for around 5 minutes or until bubbling.

5. Blend cashew nuts and water together to make a smooth cream, add to pot.

6. Gently mix in remaining ingredients.

7. Check heat and salt for your taste and add more salt/chilli as required.

8. Garnish with some fresh green herbs.

This dish is also great with some green vegetables added like steamed broccoli or spinach.

Poppy Seeds

These are a nice dark garnish that can transform the visual appearance of a dish. Great when a dish needs some form of contrast.

I tried a similar dish at an Indian restaurant one night and decided to do this much healthier version that was not loaded with cream. Mushrooms are amazing vegetables. Well for the 50% of the population who like them. I love mushrooms and my wife Verity dislikes them. This is great as she always fishes out her ones and puts them on my plate!

Mushroom Bhaji

MAKES 6 X 1 CUP SERVES

150g (5oz) button mushrooms quartered

1 tablespoon oil

1 tablespoon ginger puree

1 large onion roughly chopped

2 cloves garlic chopped or crushed

1 teaspoon garam masala

1 teaspoon ground turmeric

3 cups hot water

400g (12oz) can chopped tomatoes

1 cup brown (crimson) lentils

2 teaspoons cornflour or arrowroot

2 tablespoons cold water

100ml (3fl oz) coconut cream

2 tablespoons honey or date puree

1 teaspoon chilli puree or pinch chilli powder

1 teaspoon salt

1 red capsicum (bell pepper) finely diced

1. Saute mushrooms, oil, ginger, onion and garlic for around 10 minutes or until clear.

2. Stir in spices and mix well.

3. Add water, tomatoes and lentils. Bring to boil, turn down and simmer for around 30 minutes or until dahl is soft.

4. Mix water and cornflour into a paste in a cup and stir in to the dish to thicken.

5. Stir in remaining ingredients.

If the canned tomatoes are chunky make sure you blend them with a stick blender before using. This way you get a smooth texture rather than liquid and chunks.

Mushrooms

Despite a portion of the population disliking them, our mushroom dishes are very popular at Revive. Do not overcook them as they will reduce down to virtually nothing. Use them fresh for best results.

In my third year at Revive I discovered smoked paprika and used it in many dishes. I love the subtle smokey flavour in this stew with moreish black-eye beans.

Spanish Bean Stew

MAKES 8 X 1 CUP SERVES

3 large potatoes washed

1 tablespoon rice bran oil

1 large onion sliced

1 tablespoon rice bran oil

2 cloves garlic chopped or crushed

2 teaspoons smoked paprika

2 x 400g (12oz) cans chopped tomatoes

1 tablespoon honey or 2 tablespoons date puree

1 teaspoon crushed chilli or 1 pinch chilli powder

400g (12oz) can black eyed beans

1 teaspoon salt

200ml (6fl oz) coconut cream

1. Cut unpeeled potatoes into 2cm (1in) cubes. Roast coated in oil at 180°C (350°F) degrees for 30 minutes until soft.

2. Saute the onion, oil and garlic until clear.

3. Mix in smoked paprika.

4. Add tomatoes, honey and chilli.

5. Add half the potato and mix everything with a stick blender so it is nice and thick.

6. Add remaining ingredients and bring up to serving temperature.

Make a double batch and pop the leftovers in the freezer. It makes a great easy dinner on a cold winter's night.

If you cannot find black-eye beans you can use black turtle beans.

Smoked Paprika

This is a delicious spice that adds a warm subtle smoky flavour. It is not hot at all. Great in hotpots, potato salads and dishes that just need a little something else.

I love our version of chilli! Originally when I tried making our own varieties of chilli they were more like stews and quite runny. So I discovered this great way to add texture and thickness by blending half the beans.

Revive Chilli

MAKES 8 X 1 CUP SERVES

¼ medium pumpkin

1 large chopped onion

2 cloves garlic chopped or crushed

1 teaspoon ginger or ginger puree

2 tablespoons oil

1 teaspoon cajun spice powder

1 pinch cayenne pepper

2 x 400g (12oz) tins tomatoes

400g (12oz) can black beans

400g (12oz) can red kidney beans

200ml (6 fl oz) coconut cream

1 red capsicum (bell pepper) finely diced

2 tablespoons honey or date puree

1 teaspoon salt

1 cup frozen corn

1. Slice off skin, de-seed and cut pumpkin into 2cm (1in) cubes and mix with 2 tablespoons oil. Put on oven tray and roast 180°C (350°F) for around 20 minutes or until just soft.

2. In a large pot saute onion, garlic, oil and ginger until clear and well cooked.

3. Add spices and salt and mix well.

4. Add tomatoes and cook until boiling, stirring well.

5. Add half of each variety of beans to the mixture and using a stick blender blend well.

6. Add remaining ingredients and bring up to heat.

7. Add cayenne pepper to taste.

8. Great served on rice, corn chips, in tacos, in burritos or anything Mexican.

If you do not have a stick blender you can do batches in your blender or food processor, or you can use a potato masher.

Stick (Hand) Blender

This is the handiest kitchen tool you can have. It can blend up items directly in pots in seconds, and requires very little cleaning up. Much easier than a food processor or blender for most things.

This is a very popular winter dish. I sometimes call it a Russian stroganoff and sometimes a Hungarian goulash However I get in trouble with Russians and Hungarians every time as they both claim it is not true to their national dish. But it is a great hotpot and the joy of owning a cafe is that you can call dishes what you like. Well you can until the mafia visits.

Mushroom Goulash

MAKES 6 X 1 CUP SERVES

1 onions finely diced

2 cloves garlic chopped or crushed

2 tablespoons rice bran oil

1 teaspoon thyme dried

200g (6oz) mushrooms sliced

2 x 400g (12oz) tins chopped tomatoes

½ teaspoon salt

1 pinch cayenne pepper

2 tablespoons honey or date puree

200ml (6fl oz) coconut cream

600g (20oz) tofu cubed

1. Saute onions, garlic, mushrooms, thyme, oil in a pot for 5 minutes until onion is clear. Lid on is best so mushrooms can sweat.

2. Add tomatoes, salt, cayenne pepper and honey. Stir until heated through and just bubbling.

3. Add coconut cream and tofu and stir in gently.

4. Taste and adjust cayenne pepper and salt as required.

This hotpot is especially delicious served on quinoa.

Optional: add some seasonal vegetables (eg. roasted sliced carrots, roasted pumpkin, red capsicum).

Garlic

This is an essential ingredient in most vegetarian meals. It adds a flavour that you cannot detect, but you know if it is not there. You can chop finely or use a garlic crusher. Do not buy those pre-prepared garlic purees as they taste terrible.

This is one of my favourite quick dinners at home. Like many other ingredients, cabbage does need some strong flavours to make it taste great. It gives a great melt-in-your mouth texture in stir fries!

Curried Cabbage Stir Fry

MAKES 4 X 1 CUP SERVES

1 large onion sliced

2 cloves garlic chopped
or crushed

2 tablespoons oil

1 tablespoon ginger puree

1 teaspoon mild
curry powder

1 teaspoon cumin seeds

1 teaspoon mustard seeds

3 cups sliced
green cabbage

1 cup frozen peas

1 red capsicum (bell
pepper) cubed

½ cup almonds
roughly chopped

½ teaspoon salt

1. In a wok or pan saute the onion, oil, garlic and ginger until clear.

2. Add spices and stir in quickly.

3. Add cabbage and cook for around 5 minutes or until cabbage is soft.

4. Stir in remaining ingredients and let peas warm up.

Cabbage reduces down with cooking so you will need a bigger pan or wok than you might think.

Green Cabbage

Though it is traditionally seen as a boring vegetable, I believe cabbage can add great texture to a dish. It makes an excellent coleslaw when raw, and is great in a stir fry when cooked.

Leftover rice in the fridge + some fresh vegetables + a can of kidney beans + a few additions and you have a delicious, nutritious healthy meal in 10 minutes. It is the ultimate quick meal. And the best part is that you will have only one pan to clean!

Kidney Bean Stir Fry

MAKES 6 X 1 CUP SERVES

1 large onion chopped

2 tablespoons oil

2 cloves garlic chopped or crushed

2 tablespoons chopped ginger or ginger puree

10 mushrooms quartered

1 red capsicum (bell pepper) finely diced

2 zucchini (courgette) roughly chopped

1 large carrot diced

1 cup frozen peas

1 tablespoon poppy seeds

½ teaspoon salt

1 tablespoon honey or date puree

1 cup cooked brown rice

400g (12oz) can red kidney beans

1. In a pan or wok saute the onion, oil , ginger and garlic for 5 minutes or until clear.

2. Add vegetables and cook until they are just cooked yet still crunchy.

3. Add remaining ingredients and toss in the pan for 2 minutes or until heated through.

4. Taste for sweetness and saltiness and adjust if necessary.

Serve with some hummus (page 147) or homemade Italian tomato sauce (page 153).

Red Kidney Beans

Available in cans or soak and cook them yourself. They add great colour to any meal and have a great flavour.

If I have limited time at home to cook a meal this one is my first choice. Quinoa cooks in around 12 minutes, and while it is cooking I assemble the other ingredients in the pan which will finish at the same time as the quinoa. Combine and you have the healthiest meal!

Quinoa Stir Fry

MAKES 4 X 1 CUP SERVES

½ cup quinoa

1 cup boiling water

2 tablespoons rice bran oil

1 large onion sliced

2 cloves garlic chopped or crushed

5 cups chopped vegetables which could include:

- red capsicum (bell pepper)
- roasted pumpkin
- roasted kumara (sweet potato)
- chopped carrots
- zucchini (courgette)
- red onion
- celery
- mushrooms

½ teaspoon salt

1 tablespoon honey or
2 tablespoons date puree

2 tablespoons soy sauce or tamari

fresh herbs for garnish

1. If using roasted vegetables, roast in the oven for around 20 minutes at 180°C (350°F) or until nearly soft.

2. Put quinoa and boiling water in a pot and bring to the boil. Turn down to around ¼ heat and simmer for 12 minutes with the lid on.

3. In a separate pan or wok saute onion, oil, garlic until clear.

4. Add all other ingredients (except quinoa) to onion mix and fry for around 5 minutes until just cooked.

5. Stir in cooked quinoa and taste.

6. Garnish with fresh herbs.

Make sure you cook up extra grains like quinoa and keep them in your fridge so you can whip up a quick meal like this one in minutes.

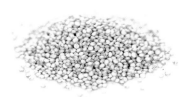

Quinoa

A high quality grain that is high in protein and cooks in under 15 minutes. Use in place of rice in most recipes. Quinoa cooks quickly however it burns easily so be careful!

In my second year at Revive we had this dish displayed as a "Black Turtle Bean Stir Fry". A new customer came in and was quite concerned that we may be using turtles in our food. He was fine when we explained we were vegetarian however our team found this very amusing.

Miso Bean Mingle

MAKES 4 X 1 CUP SERVES

8 frozen spinach balls (around 2 cups)

1 large onion finely diced

2 cloves garlic chopped or crushed

1 tablespoon ginger puree

1 tablespoon rice bran oil

½ red capsicum (bell pepper) finely diced

½ can or 1 cup frozen whole kernel corn

2 tablespoons miso paste

½ cup hot water

1 cup cooked brown rice

400g (12oz) can azuki beans (or black turtle or black eye beans)

½ teaspoon black sesame seeds

½ teaspoon white sesame seeds

1. Soak the frozen spinach balls in a bowl with very hot water to soften.

2. In a frying pan cook the oil, onion, garlic and ginger until the onion is clear (around 5 minutes).

3. Add remaining ingredients (except sesame seeds) and mix for around 5 minutes until heated through.

4. Garnish with black and white sesame seeds.

Miso

Miso is a Japanese ingredient made from fermented soy beans. It is very good for your digestion and has a nice salty flavour. It is available at all Asian supermarkets. There are several types you can get. Any will be fine for this recipe.

A great casual meal when you have to feed a lot of people. Just lay out all the ingredients and everyone can design their own as they wish. This is also great for a quick healthy meal.

Super Nachos

MAKES 4 X 1 CUP SERVES

CHILLI BEANS

1 can chilli beans

1 can baked beans

1 onion chopped

2 cloves garlic chopped or crushed

1 cup frozen corn

1 tablespoon oil

1 teaspoon cornflour or arrowroot

1 tablespoon cold water

OTHER INGREDIENTS

1 bag triangle corn chips

1 carrot grated

3 tomatoes cubed

1 yellow capsicum (bell pepper)

fresh green lettuce

hummus (page 147)

1. Select a large pot and saute the onion, garlic and oil for around 5 minutes or until clear.

2. Add baked beans, chilli beans and corn and stir until bubbling.

3. Mix together the cornflour and water and pour in the mix to thicken, stirring for around 30 seconds.

4. Layer your plate with corn chips, chilli beans and the vegetables.

5. Finish with a generous spoonful of hummus.

You can add almost any fresh salad vegetable to this mix.

Corn Chips

These are a great base for many meals. Made from corn they are a whole grain food. I prefer the natural flavours and avoid flavour enhancers which are in most brands. They are also great as a garnish pushed in the top of a stir fry or curry.

These are our hot meals at Revive that are not classed as hotpots! They typically take a little longer and more skill to make but are worth the effort.

Main Meals

Introduced in our sixth year these quickly became a hit with our regular customers. We tried large and small sizes and settled on an eighth cup size balls with 3 served per person. However you can make the balls as small or as large as you like.

Meatless Meatballs

**MAKES 30 BALLS
(10 SERVES)**

2 large potatoes

4 cloves of garlic squeezed or chopped

1 large onion finely chopped

2 teaspoons rice bran oil

2 cups fine rolled oats

1 teaspoon dry mixed herbs

½ cup grated carrot

½ cup soy sauce/tamari

½ cup chickpea (besan) flour

½ cup soy/rice milk

4 cups Italian tomato sauce (page 153)

1 packet wholemeal spaghetti cooked as per instructions or brown rice

1. Boil potatoes until soft, drain and mash.

2. Mix potato and all other ingredients (except tomato sauce and spaghetti) together well.

3. Form into balls ($\frac{1}{8}$ cup each) and put on a lightly oiled baking tray.

4. Bake at 150°C (300°F) for 40 minutes or until cooked right through.

5. Cover meatballs with tomato sauce (warm up first if you are using from fridge or freezer).

6. Serve on spaghetti or rice with a sprinkling of fresh green herbs.

You can make these balls in advance and keep in refrigerator or freezer and warm up and add the tomato sauce before serving.

You can use wholemeal flour for these if you do not have chickpea flour.

Wholemeal Pasta

Do not give your body poor quality food and miss out on all the fibre and nutrients - choose wholemeal pastas over white pastas. Many supermarkets and most health stores stock a great range of pasta made from wholemeal flour. It takes a similar time to cook as white.

I ordered a take-out vegetarian burrito from a Mexican cafe one day and it was not until I was in my car a few blocks away that I discovered they had accidentally made a chicken one. I reluctantly ate around the chicken but thought I could make something similar to this - and here it is.

Not Chicken Burritos

MAKES 6

600g (19oz) pack firm tofu

3 cups cubed pumpkin

2 tablespoons rice bran oil

1 large onion finely sliced

1 stalk celery finely diced

1 green capsicum (bell pepper) diced

½ teaspoon salt

3 tablespoons sweet chilli sauce

6 x large burritos (tortilla flat bread)

optional: 1 pinch cayenne pepper for garnish

1. Ahead of time take your tofu, drain it, and store in your freezer for at least 2 days. It will change into a nice chicken-like texture. Defrost and slice into strips.

2. De-skin and chop pumpkin into 2cm (1in) cubes and roast for 15 minutes with oil at 180°C (350°F) or until just soft.

3. Saute onion, 1 tablespoon of oil and celery in a pan for 5 minutes or until clear but still firm.

4. Add tofu strips and green capsicum and fry until tofu hardens up slightly.

5. Add remaining ingredients and mix. Taste test.

6. Place 1 cup of the mixture in middle of burrito, bring sides in first and wrap.

7. Oil top of burritos and garnish with cayenne pepper.

8. Bake for 10 minutes at 180°C (350°F) to crisp them up.

Delicious served with a salad and/or pineapple salsa (page 148).

Cayenne Pepper

An excellent ingredient for a bit of heat, however in this dish it is used as a garnish for a nice dark red colour. Cayenne is also excellent for blood circulation. If you have poor circulation or would like to get your blood moving when you are sick put some in your socks before you go to bed.

I love baked potatoes - however the most important thing is to have a good hotpot-style sauce to go over them and some kind of healthy cream.

Baked Potato with Chickpea Korma

MAKES 4 X 1 CUP SERVES

8 large washed potatoes (un-peeled)

1 large onion diced

1 tablespoon rice bran oil

2 cloves garlic crushed or chopped

1 teaspoon ground cumin

1 teaspoon ground coriander

1 teaspoon ground turmeric

2 x 400g (12oz) cans chopped tomatoes

2 tablespoons honey or date puree

200ml (6fl oz) coconut cream

400g (12oz) can chickpeas (garbanzo beans)

1 teaspoon salt

sunflower cream (page 146)

VEGETABLE OPTIONS

- lettuce
- canned beetroot
- chopped tomato
- chopped cucumber
- grated carrot
- coleslaw

1. Place whole potatoes on a baking tray and brush lightly with oil. Bake for 1-2 hours at 150°C (300°F). Time will vary depending on their size.

2. In a pan saute onion, garlic and oil for around 5 minutes until clear.

3. Add spices and mix in for around 30 seconds.

4. Add blended tomatoes and bring back to boil.

5. Add honey, chickpeas, coconut cream and salt.

6. Cut a cross in the top of the potatoes and squeeze the base so it opens like a flower.

7. Top with korma, fresh vegetables and sunflower cream.

These are very quick and easy to make once you have made them a couple of times. They are one of my top meals to create in a couple of minutes.

Curried Zucchini Fritters

MAKES 20 SMALL OR 10 LARGE FRITTERS

1 medium onion finely diced

3 zucchini (courgette)

1 cup chickpea (besan) flour

optional ½ cup water

1 teaspoon salt

1 tablespoon sweet chilli sauce

1 tablespoon black sesame seeds

1 teaspoon mild curry powder

rice bran oil for frying

1. Saute the onion in a little oil until clear.

2. Grate the zucchini with a hand grater using the largest holes.

3. Mix all the ingredients together in a mixing bowl. The moisture from the zucchini should make everything the right consistency however you may need to add up to half a cup of water.

4. Let the mixture sit for around 20 minutes in the fridge, then stir again. If you are in a rush this is not absolutely necessary but you will end up with a more consistent mix that will stick together better.

5. Fry with a little oil in a hot pan (ideally non-stick) for around 4-5 minutes each side or until golden brown and cooked right through.

6. Serve immediately with sweet chilli sauce, salsa or chutney on the side.

You can substitute wholemeal flour for the chickpea flour in this recipe.

When making fritters I make a test one first to check flavour, the heat of the pan and that everything sticks together.

Chickpea (Besan) Flour

Available from good Indian stores and whole food stores. This is my favourite flour. It is great for patties, fritters, pizza bases and can be used in many places instead of wheat flour. It can also be called Chana Flour.

I love getting a traditional meal and making a healthy version. This is a healthy meat-less meat loaf. The tomato sauce is what makes it special!

Neat Loaf

MAKES 8 SERVES

½ cup brown lentils

2 cups boiling water

1 cup fine rolled oats

1 onion finely diced

2 cloves garlic crushed

¼ cup soy sauce or tamari

1 teaspoon salt

1 cup cottage cheese or 300g (10oz) mashed tofu

up to ½ cup water

1 teaspoon sage

1 teaspoon oregano

2 carrots grated

1 red capsicum (bell pepper) finely diced

3 cups Italian tomato sauce (page 153)

1. Cook the lentils in the water for around 30 minutes or until soft. Drain so there is no liquid.

2. In a bowl mix all ingredients (except tomato sauce). You should have a sticky mixture. You may need to add some water if it is dry.

3. Press into a lightly oiled oven tray - approximately 3cm (1½in) deep.

4. Pour over 1 cup of the tomato sauce.

5. Bake for 40 minutes at 150°C (300°F) or until firm.

6. Cover with the remaining tomato sauce.

7. Cut into squares and serve so the tomato sauce cascades over the neat loaf.

Brown (Crimson) Lentils

A great meaty style lentil. Goes very well with dried or fresh sage. Good for lasagnes, stews and many dishes where you may usually use mince meat. Crimson lentils are the best variety of brown lentils.

Tofu on its own is boring and bland, however it soaks up flavour magnificently. This dish is not a meal in itself but is a good accompaniment or perhaps useful for open sandwiches or a salad ingredient.

Honey & Soy Tofu Steaks

MAKES 4-8 SERVES

300g (10oz) pack firm tofu

2 tablespoons rice bran oil

4 tablespoons liquid honey

1 tablespoon finely chopped ginger or ginger puree

2 tablespoons soy sauce or tamari

4 tablespoons warm water

1 spring onion (scallion)

black and white sesame seeds for garnish

liquid honey for garnish

1. Heat a large non-stick frying pan and coat with oil.

2. Cut the tofu into slabs around 2cm (1in) thick.

3. Cook the tofu strips on high heat for around 5 minutes each side - they should firm up a little and darken slightly. This may take a little longer depending on how much water is in your tofu. If necessary drain out the water.

4. Mix together the marinade of honey, ginger, soy sauce and water and pour over the tofu, ensuring it is coated evenly.

5. Cook for around 3 minutes per side or until they turn golden brown. Ideally the liquid should just be drying out as you finish cooking.

6. Serve garnished with spring onions, sesame seeds and a couple of squiggles of liquid honey.

The best way to infuse flavour into tofu is not to marinate it. It is best by heating it up like in this recipe and then the heat draws in the flavour.

Honey

A great natural sweetener. Can be used in place of sugar for most recipes and is a great garnish drizzled over the top of many dishes.

This is a popular dish that is one of my all time favourite meals at Revive.

Spanikopita

SERVES 6

2 onions sliced

3 cloves crushed garlic

1 tablespoon rice bran oil

500g (16oz) pack spinach frozen (preferably whole leaves)

12 free range eggs beaten

200g (6 oz) feta cheese cubed

1 teaspoon salt

4 tablespoons rice bran oil for brushing

1 teaspoon black poppy seeds for garnish

150g (5oz) filo (very fine) pastry

1. In a pan, saute onions, garlic and oil until clear.

2. Defrost spinach in hot water. Drain well.

3. In a bowl mix onion mix, spinach, eggs, feta and salt.

4. In shallow oven tray, layer filo on the bottom, up the sides and hanging over the edge. Brush a little oil, repeat for 6 layers - switch direction of each sheet so there is overlap.

5. Pour in the spinach and egg mix.

6. Add 3 layers of filo pastry on top. Roll the overlapping filo together to form a crust. Make sure there is a good brushing of oil on top.

7. Sprinkle poppy seeds on top.

8. Bake at 150°C (300°F) for approximately 30-40 minutes or until just set. The cooking time varies depending on the depth of the mix.

9. Cut into squares and serve with a chutney.

Frozen Spinach

Spinach is a great vegetable, however it is often expensive in the winter. It also reduces down to a tenth the size you started with. Having frozen spinach in your freezer is a convenient way to use this great vegetable in your meals. You can buy either chopped or whole leaf.

These are tasty cakes. You can make them large size for a meal or small size for finger snacks.

Pumpkin Risotto Cake

MAKES AROUND 10 CAKES

1 cup short grain brown rice

2 cups boiling water

2 tablespoons rice bran oil

3 cups pumpkin roasted until soft

½ cup chickpea (chana/besan) flour

½ teaspoon salt

2 teaspoons mild curry powder

½ teaspoon fennel seeds

½ cup water

1 teaspoon chilli puree

1 teaspoon black sesame seeds

1. Cook rice and water for around 40 minutes until soft and sticky.

2. Mix up all ingredients in a mixing bowl.

3. Adjust mixture so it is sticky but not sloppy. Add water if it is too dry, add chickpea flour if it is too sloppy.

4. Spoon out ½ cup mixtures and carefully place on oiled oven tray.

5. Garnish with sesame seeds.

6. Bake for 30 minutes at 180°C/350°F.

Serve with a plum sauce, sweet chilli sauce or chutney.

Optional: add 200g (6oz) crumbled tofu to the mix for protein.

Black Sesame Seeds

I love these crunchy little black seeds. The high contrast can transform a dish instantly. Works particularly well with yellow food and especially Asian dishes.

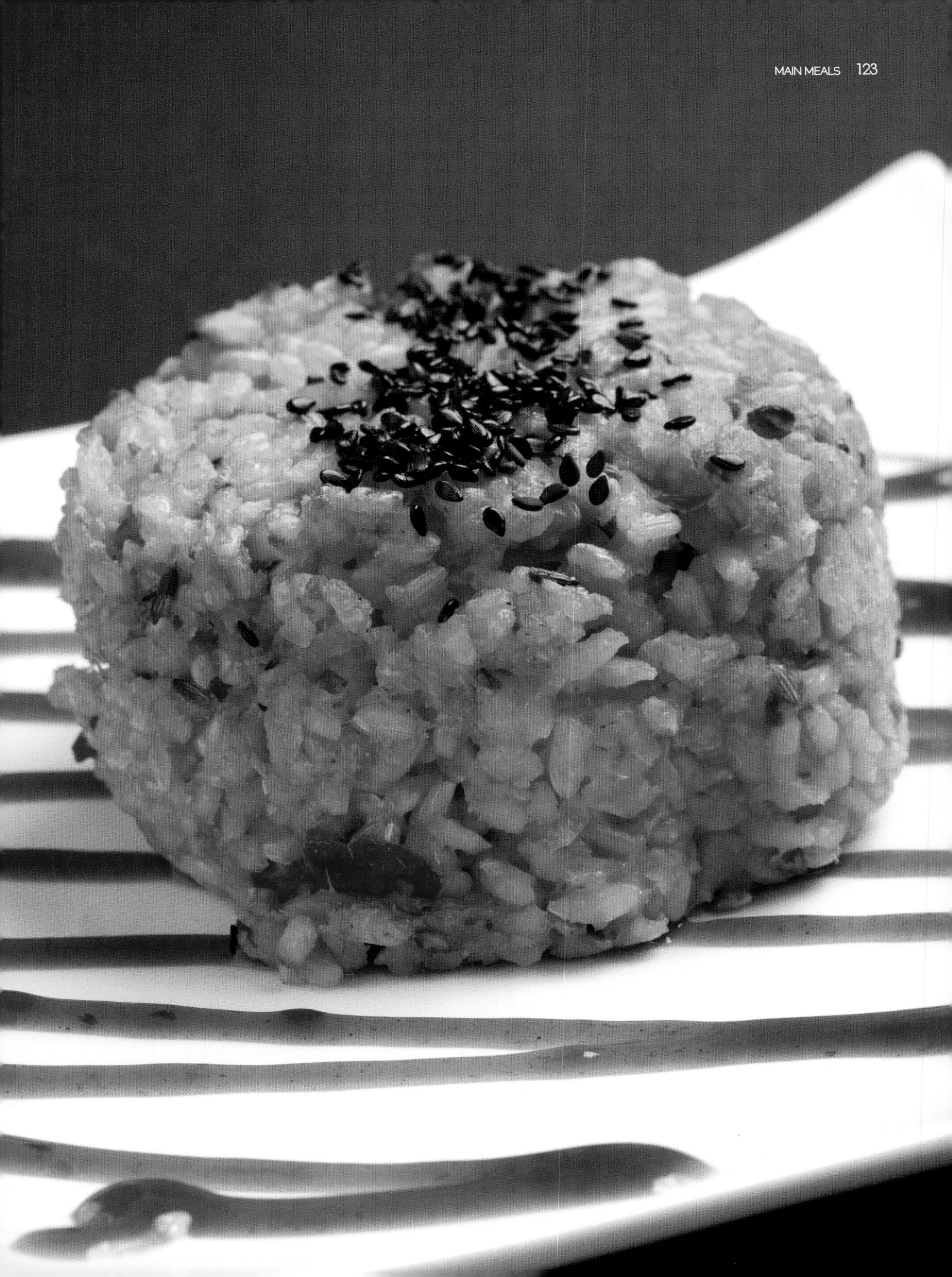

A dish we sold at Revive every day in our first year.
It is easy to make however it does need a little time to
roast off the vegetables.

Pumpkin & Kumara Balls

**MAKES 8 LARGE OR
16 SMALL BALLS**

¼ large pumpkin peeled
and cut into cubes

2 medium kumara (sweet
potato) cut into cubes

2 tablespoons oil

½ teaspoon salt

2 cloves crushed garlic

1 large onion diced finely

2 teaspoons cumin

2 tablespoons
pumpkin seeds

½ cup white sesame seeds

1. Roast the pumpkin & kumara with the salt and oil for around 30 minutes at 180°C (350°F) or until just cooked.

2. Saute onions and garlic in a little oil until clear.

3. Mix onions and roasted vegetables with the cumin and pumpkin seeds. Use your hands and squish it all together so it binds.

4. Roll into balls with your hands. You can make either large or bite sized.

5. Roll in sesame seeds and put onto an oiled oven tray.

6. Bake for 30 minutes at 150 °C (300°F) or until golden brown.

Serve with brown rice and satay sauce (page 152).

Undercook the vegetables slightly so you get a firm mix. If you overcook the ingredients they can be mushy.

White Sesame Seeds

A staple garnish ingredient to have in the cupboard. They work especially well with anything Asian, green or yellow. They have a nice flavour when toasted.

A delicious pasta and tomato dish with a great ingredient ... mushrooms. Cannelloni is one of our standard dishes at Revive and features most weeks. We make mushroom, spinach, chickpea and roasted vegetables varieties.

Mushroom Cannelloni

MAKES 6

2 tablespoons rice bran oil

200g (6oz) mushrooms sliced

600g (19oz) firm tofu mashed

2 cups onion jam (page 155) or 1 lightly sauted onion

1 teaspoon dried thyme

½ teaspoon salt

parsley for garnish

1 packet fresh lasagne sheets

4 cups Italian tomato sauce (page 153)

1. Saute oil and mushrooms in a pan for around 5 minutes.

2. Mix the above with mashed tofu, onion jam, thyme and salt in a bowl.

3. Cut pasta sheets into strips so they measure approximately 100 x 200 mm (4 x 8 inches). Lay them out on your bench.

4. Place ½ cup mushroom mix in the middle of a pasta strip. Fold the side closest to you over the top, and roll on the piece remaining.

5. Spread 1 cup Italian tomato sauce over the base of an oven tray. Place the cannelloni gently in the tray. Cover liberally with more Italian tomato sauce.

6. Bake at 150°C/300°F for 40 minutes.

If you are not into tofu, you can replace it with cottage cheese.

Wholemeal Pasta Sheets

These can be hard to find but are great for making any pasta dish. Just wrap up your filling and bake with some tomato sauce. They can come fresh (soft) and shelf stable(hard). If your lasagne sheets are hard, simply brush on a little water so you can fold them.

This is a great winter dish and hits the spot when the weather is really cold and you want something hearty. On the menu most weeks during winter.

Shepherdess Pie

SERVES 6-8

BASE:

1 cup brown lentils

3 cups water

1 large onion finely diced

1 teaspoon dried sage

1 teaspoon salt

2 cups Italian tomato sauce
(page 153)

TOPPING:

3 large potatoes steamed
and mashed

1 tablespoon sweet chilli sauce

1 teaspoon whole grain mustard

1 teaspoon ground turmeric

1 teaspoon salt

1 cup soy or rice milk

1. Cook lentils and water for around 30 minutes or until soft. Drain if any water left.

2. In a bowl mix the lentils together with other base ingredients.

3. In another bowl, mix all topping ingredients together.

4. Select a flat lasagne style dish, lay base mix in.

5. Spread potato topping on top.

6. Bake 150°C (300°F) for 30 minutes.

This dish may be quite runny when just cooked - so either serve from the dish you cook in, or if you refrigerate it will firm up.

Sage

Dried Sage is an excellent herb that goes well with lentils.

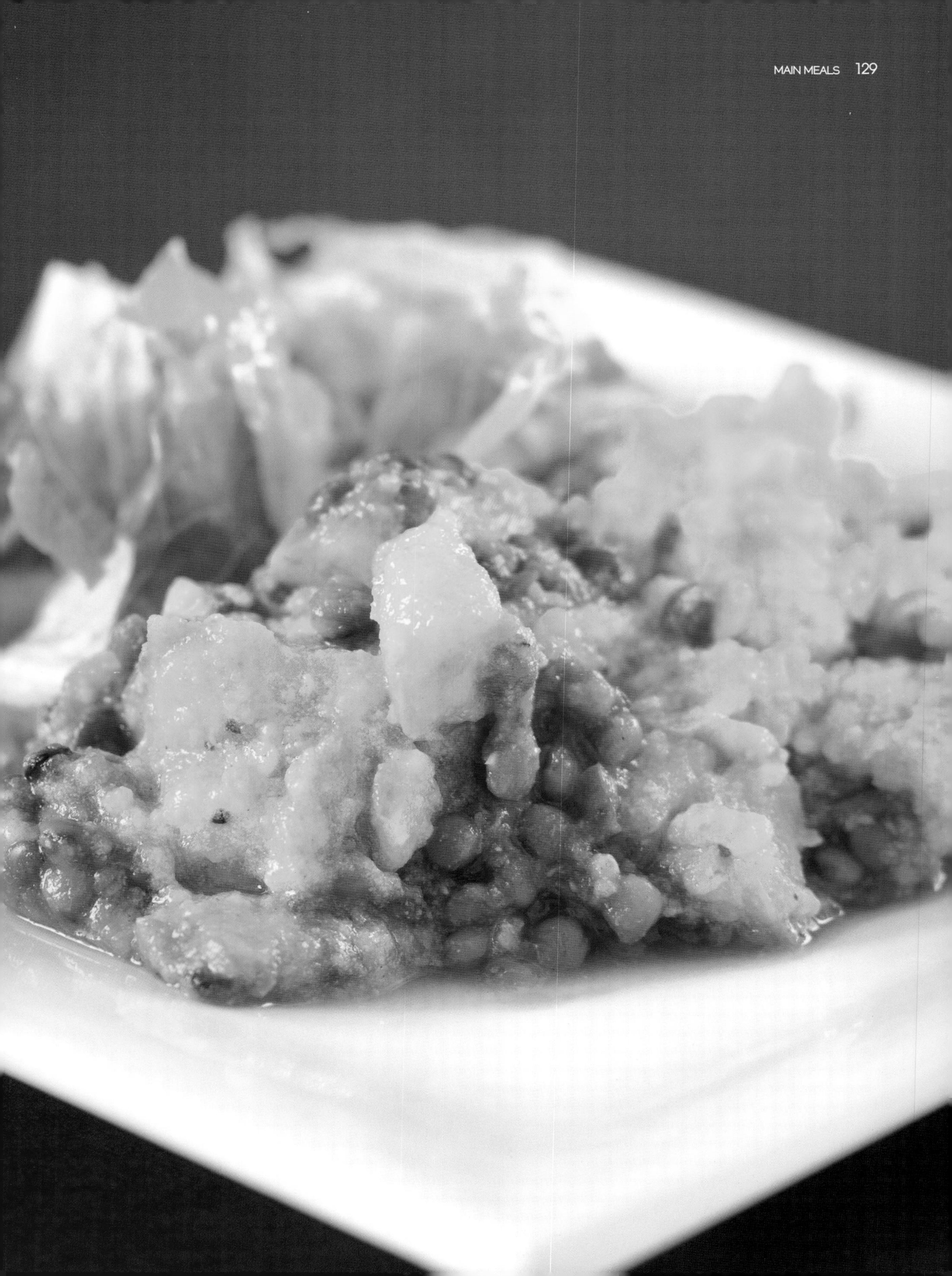

We started Mexican bean burritos at Revive in 2007 and they were really popular - but as with anything popular people start getting too much of a good thing. So I started to look for some more fillings and in my experimentation this one came up as a good favourite.

Indian Potato & Chickpea Wraps

MAKES 6

3 large potatoes

6 large burritos (tortilla flat bread)

1 large onion sliced thinly

1 tablespoon oil

400g (12oz) can chickpeas (garbanzo beans) drained

1 teaspoon cumin seeds

1 teaspoon ground cumin

½ teaspoon ground turmeric

1 teaspoon garam masala

2 tablespoons date puree or honey

1 teaspoon salt

1 cup frozen peas

oil for brushing

½ cup fresh coriander (cilantro) chopped

1 teaspoon black sesame seeds

1. Preheat oven to 180°C (350°F).

2. Cut potato into cubes and cook for around 10-15 minutes in boiling water until soft. Drain and mash roughly.

3. Fry onion and oil until clear in a separate pan.

4. Add spices to onion and cook for around 1 more minute stirring regularly.

5. Combine all ingredients (except burritos). Reserve some cumin seeds and sesame seeds for garnish.

6. Place 1 cup of the mixture in middle of burrito, bring sides in first and wrap.

7. Brush with a little oil and add some extra sesame seeds and cumin seeds on top for garnish.

8. Bake for 10 minutes at 180°F (350°F) to crisp them up.

Coriander (Cilantro)

A very flavoursome and fragrant herb that makes a great garnish. Goes well with anything curried or spicy. If possible add near the end of a recipe when you are about to serve so it stays green. Best chopped roughly. You can grow it in your garden but it does go to seed easily.

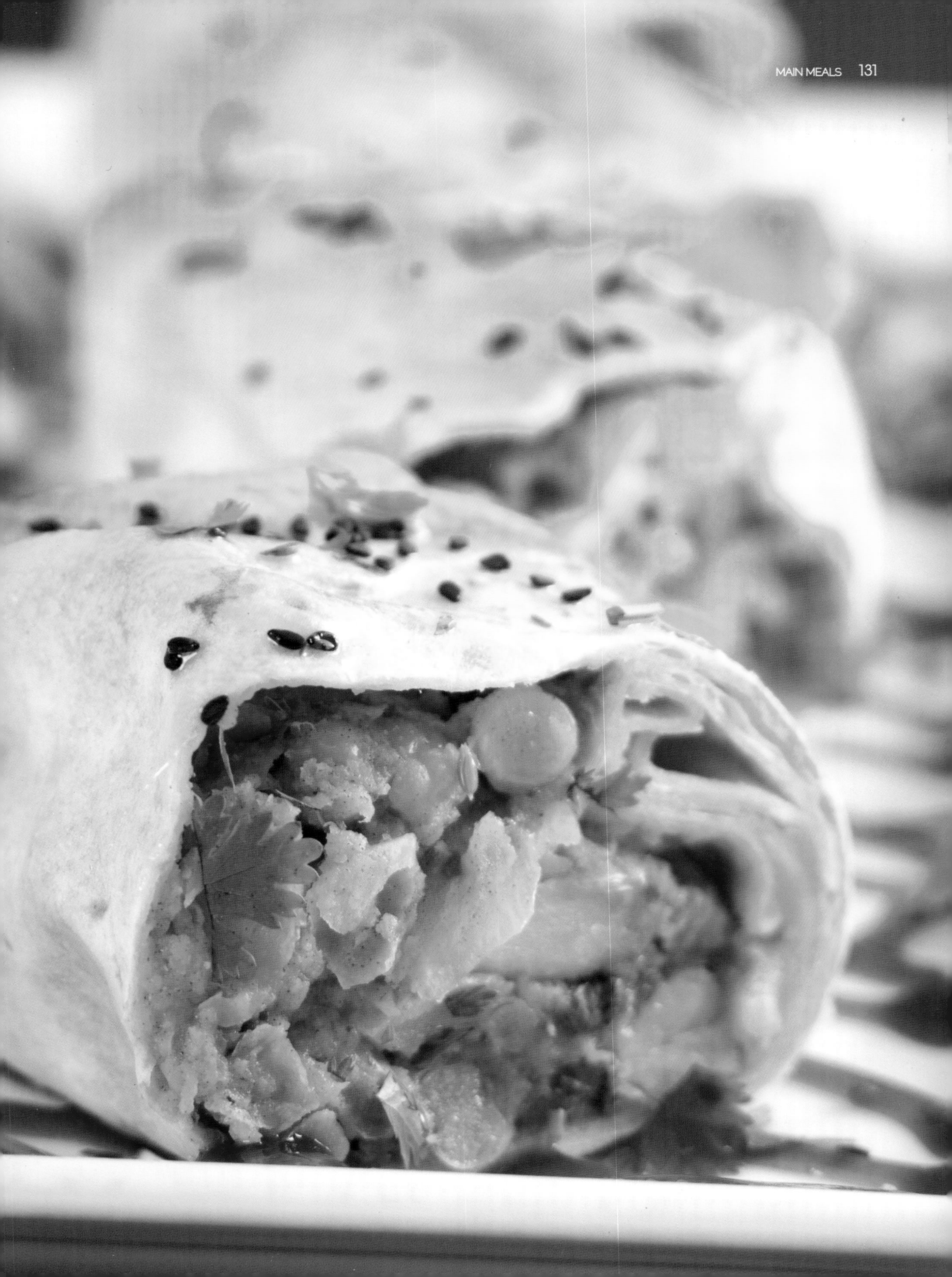

This is a great cholesterol-free scrambled eggs substitute. The turmeric is great in making the boring grey colour of tofu an appetising yellow. When we did breakfasts in our first two years of Revive this dish was a hit.

Scrambled Tofu with Mushrooms

MAKES 3 X 1 CUP SERVES

1 tablespoon rice bran oil

2 cloves garlic chopped or crushed

½ red onion finely sliced

1 teaspoon chopped ginger or ginger puree

300g (10oz) tofu crumbled

2 tomatoes finely diced

12 button mushrooms chopped in half

2 tablespoons soy sauce or tamari

¼ teaspoon ground turmeric

1. Cook onion, oil, ginger, mushrooms and garlic for around 3-5 minutes or until onion is clear.

2. Add tofu and cook for another 3 minutes stirring regularly.

3. Add remaining ingredients to pan and mix.

4. Serve on fresh whole grain toast with tomatoes and a sprinkle of fresh parsley.

Red Onion

Great for adding a dark purple colour to meals. Use raw or if cooking, only cook lightly so it does not lose its colour.

A classic winter dish. You cannot go wrong with soups. All you need are vegetables, some flavour, and serve with some whole grain bread!

Soups

This may look like an unassuming soup but it is delicious.
And great in winter when carrots are big and inexpensive!

Carrot & Coriander Soup

MAKES 8 X 1 CUP SERVES

2 onions roughly chopped

2 cloves garlic chopped
or crushed

1 tablespoon rice bran oil

5 large carrots
roughly chopped

½ teaspoon ground nutmeg

3 teaspoons
ground coriander

1 teaspoon ground cumin

4 cups hot water

4 tablespoons date puree
or honey

1 teaspoon salt

1 cup raw cashew nuts

1 cup cold water

2 carrots grated

1. Cook onion, garlic and oil until clear (but not coloured).

2. Add carrots, nutmeg, coriander, cumin and water and simmer until carrots are soft (approximately 30 minutes).

3. Add salt and date puree. Blend well with a stick blender.

4. Using a blender or stick blender in a separate container, blend cashews and cold water together. Add to carrot mixture.

5. Taste for sweetness and saltiness, modify if necessary.

6. Add grated carrot just before serving for texture.

If your carrots are fresh and clean you will not have to peel them.
Save time and get a higher yield!

Coriander

A great spice that is actually quite sweet and can be used in sweet dishes as well. A top spice to have in your cupboard.

It is very easy to make, and is made creamy by the addition of a cashew puree. This adds taste and creaminess (without dairy). It also adds protein, so it is a "complete protein" when eaten with wholemeal bread.

Creamy Tomato Soup

MAKES 7 x 1 CUP SERVES

2 tablespoons rice bran oil

1 large onion chopped

1 stalk celery
roughly chopped

1 small carrot
roughly chopped

2 cloves garlic chopped
or crushed

3 x 400g (12oz) cans
tomatoes

2 cups hot water

½ teaspoon salt

1 tablespoon honey or
date puree

½ teaspoon mixed herbs

1 cup raw cashew nuts

1 cup cold water

1. Saute vegetables, garlic and oil until onion is clear.

2. Add all remaining ingredients (except cashew nuts and cold water). Bring to boil then simmer for 20 minutes to let the flavours mingle.

3. Blend well with stick blender.

4. Make cashew cream with cashews, water and a stick blender and stir in.

Make a quadruple batch of any soup and put in your freezer - you will be thankful on a cold winters night when you arrive home and can have dinner in a short time!

You can use almonds instead of cashews for the cream if you like.

Italian Mixed Herbs

Fresh herbs are always the best option. However having some mixed herbs in your pantry is a great alternative. The go especially well with tomato. "Mixed Herbs" is just a mix of various herbs and every mix is different. A typical mix may contain oregano, basil, sage, rosemary, and thyme.

Pumpkin Soup takes a little more prep but the end result is worth it. It would have to be the world's most loved soup. I wanted a soup that was more than just "pumpkin" so added some Thai curry paste to give it some great flavour.

Creamy Thai Pumpkin Soup

MAKES 8 X 1 CUP SERVES

2 large onions

2 cloves garlic chopped or crushed

1 tablespoon ginger puree

1 tablespoon oil

½ medium pumpkin skinned and cubed

6 cups hot water

1 pinch cayenne pepper

1 tablespoon Thai red curry paste

1 cup coconut cream

4 tablespoons date puree or honey

1 teaspoon salt

1. In a large pot saute onion, garlic, ginger and oil until onion is clear.

2. Add pumpkin, water and simmer until pumpkin is soft (approximately 30 minutes).

3. Blend very well with stick blender.

4. Add remaining ingredients. Stir and adjust for sweet and salty.

You can put the whole pumpkin in the oven and cook for an hour at 180°C (350°F) and let it cool. It will then be a breeze to cut off the skin and cube.

Pumpkin

What a fabulous sweet and soft vegetable. Available mostly in winter. Great for soups, or as an addition to many salads. Lovely when roasted with a little oil and salt.

This is a cross between a dahl and a soup. I try lots of different things at Revive and did not think it would sell that well, but I gave it a go and this soup is very popular when we have it on the menu.

Indian Spiced Lentil Soup

MAKES 8 X 1 CUP SERVES

1 large chopped onion

2 cloves garlic chopped or crushed

2 tablespoons oil

1 teaspoon ground cumin

1 teaspoon ground turmeric

1 teaspoon mild curry powder

1 stalk celery roughly chopped

1 large carrot roughly chopped

400g (12oz) can tomatoes blended

1 cup red lentils

6 cups hot water

1 cup cashew nuts

1 cup cold water

1 teaspoon salt

4 tablespoons date puree or honey

1. Saute onion, garlic and oil until clear.

2. Stir in spices and vegetables.

3. Add lentils, tomatoes and water and bring to boil. Simmer for around 30 minutes or until lentils and vegetables are cooked.

4. Blend with a stick blender.

5. Separately blend cashew nuts and cold water to make a thick cream. Add to the pot.

6. Add salt and date puree and taste.

Ensure salt is added at end, not earlier, as it will inhibit the lentils cooking properly.

Canned Tomatoes

A great product that you can keep in the cupboard and add when required. Come in many thicknesses, however in most cases you are best to blend with a stick blender so you have a smooth texture.

This section is the flavour powerhouse of our cafe. These bases, dressings and ingredients are usually prepped the day before and ready to add to dishes to give them awesome flavour. Add some of these ingredients to your fridge to spice up your dishes!

Flavour Boosters

This is a great healthy alternative to sour cream. You will be surprised how delicious it is.

Sunflower Cream

¾ cup water

1 cup sunflower seeds

¼ cup lemon juice

1 teaspoon onion powder

½ teaspoon salt

1. Combine all ingredients in a food processer or blender.

2. Blend well until smooth.

3. You may have to add a little more water so the blender keeps everything turning. However only add a little bit at a time as it can easily get too runny.

Optional: add a pinch of cayenne pepper to the mixture and/or as a garnish.

This cream will go grey with time so best to use it the day it is made.

This is my favourite dip of all time - I always have chickpeas in the freezer so I can whip it up at a moments notice.

Classic Hummus

2 x 400g (12oz) cans of chickpeas (garbanzo beans)

½ teaspoon of salt

2 cloves of garlic chopped or crushed

2 tablespoons tahini (ground hulled sesame seed paste)

¼ cup rice bran oil

¼ cup water

4 tablespoons lemon juice

1. Put all ingredients in food processor and blend until smooth. You can also use a stick blender or a regular blender however you may have to add more water to keep it flowing.

2. Taste. Note that all batches vary in flavour as salt, chickpeas and lemon juice always have different flavours and consistency.

3. Add water/oil/salt as needed. You should be able to taste every ingredient slightly, with not too much of any ingredient coming through.

I prefer rice bran oil. Olive oil has a strong flavour and tends to be overpowering. You can adjust the level of oil and replace with water for a lower fat option.

A quick and easy to make accompaniment to nachos, burritos or as a dip for crackers or vegetable sticks. This salsa is a hit at all my cooking classes and seems to go with any meal.

Pineapple Salsa

MAKES 2 CUPS

500g (16oz) can crushed pineapple (in own juice) drained

½ red capsicum (bell pepper)

½ red onion

3 tablespoons freshly squeezed lemon juice

1 small bunch of coriander (cilantro) - finely chopped (or parsley if not available)

sprinkle of cayenne pepper (optional)

1. Finely dice onion, capsicum and coriander.

2. Combine all ingredients in a mixing bowl.

This salsa is best made fresh. It does not taste the same the next day.

A beautiful sprinkle for any meal or salad - especially the roast potato salad.

Almond Dukkah

MAKES 1 CUP

1 tablespoon rice bran oil

1 cup almonds

1 tablespoon cumin seeds

2 tablespoons coriander seeds

½ tablespoon fennel seeds

1 tablespoon sesame seeds

1. Put all ingredients onto an oven tray and bake at 180°C (350°F) for 5 minutes.

2. Let the mixture cool slightly.

3. Place in a food processor and blend very briefly until slightly blended but not into dust. You want a mixture of nut dust and uneven pieces.

4. This will keep for many weeks in a sealed, air-tight container in the refrigerator.

You can use cashews or any combination of nuts for this recipe.

This is a great eggless aioli that we use in some salads at Revive. It can transform a boring salad instantly. It is high in fat so you do need to use sparingly.

Revive Aioli

MAKES 3 CUPS

½ cup soy or rice milk

1 tablespoon cider vinegar

3 cloves garlic

1 tablespoon whole grain mustard

½ teaspoon salt

2 cups rice bran oil

½ to 1 cup room temperature water

1. Select a blender, food processor or stick blender.

2. Blend all ingredients (except oil and water).

3. While blending, slowly add oil and then add water at end until desired consistency is reached.

When making dressings you need to ensure that all items are at room temperature, and that you add the oil slowly. Otherwise the dressing may "split" where the oil and other ingredients do not combine and you end up with an ugly mess. If this does happen do not throw it out - but start again with your base mix and slowly pour in your split dressing.

While not an ingredient in aioli, add 1 tablespoon of sweet chilli sauce to bump up the flavour.

Will keep in the refrigerator for up to a month.

I am always searching for new and nice dressings. This is a Moroccan-based dressing and seems to go well with everything. It is a fusion of some great spices.

Chermoula Dressing

MAKES 2 CUPS

½ teaspoon salt

1 tablespoon cider vinegar

3 cloves garlic

2 tablespoons honey or date puree

2 teaspoons ground cumin

2 teaspoons ground turmeric

1 teaspoon crushed chilli

1 cup rice bran oil

¼ cup room temperature water

2 teaspoons cumin seeds (optional)

1.   Select a blender, food processor or stick blender.

2.   Blend all ingredients (except oil, water and seeds).

3.   While blending, slowly add oil and then add water at end until desired consistency is reached.

4.   Mix in cumin seeds.

Will keep in the refrigerator for up to a month.

This is a great sauce that tastes extra tangy because of the ginger. It goes well on many dishes, in salads and is great on noodles, potatoes or tofu.

Satay Sauce

MAKES 3 CUPS

1 large onion roughly chopped

2 tablespoons crushed or finely chopped ginger

2 cloves garlic finely chopped

2 tablespoons rice bran oil

2 teaspoons ground cumin

1 teaspoon ground turmeric

1 teaspoon ground coriander

1 cup peanut butter

2 cups hot water

½ cup date puree or 4 tablespoons honey

½ teaspoon salt

optional - ½ teaspoon crushed chilli or 2 tablespoons sweet chilli sauce

1. In a pot, saute onions, garlic, ginger and oil for 10 minutes or until clear.

2. Add spices and quickly stir in (do not let burn).

3. Mix in peanut butter, water, date puree and salt.

4. Stir until mixture starts to bubble and remove from heat.

5. Blend the mixture with a stick blender.

6. Taste and add salt/chilli as necessary.

7. Add more water if you want a thinner mixture.

This is our simple Italian tomato sauce that goes in, under or over so many dishes at Revive. Always have some in your freezer or fridge for a delicious instant meal.

Italian Tomato Sauce

MAKES 6 CUPS

1 large onion

4 cloves garlic crushed

2 tablespoons rice bran oil

3 x 400g (12oz) tins tomatoes

¾ teaspoon salt

1 teaspoon mixed dried herbs

3 tablespoons honey or date puree

1. In a pot, saute onion, garlic and oil until clear.

2. Add remaining ingredients and cook until bubbling.

3. Blend all of the sauce with a stick blender.

If you really like garlic add 3 times as much for a great garlic taste.

This is our main sweetener at Revive. Date Puree can be used instead of sugar to sweeten most dishes. Honey is my second preference for sweetening - however its cost is significantly more than dates.

Date Puree

MAKES 2 CUPS

2 cups pitted dried dates

2 cups boiling water

1. Put dates in boiling water for 5 minutes to soften.

2. Put all water and dates in blender and blend well until you have a smooth paste.

3. If you hear date stones (as they occasionally come through), sieve the puree.

4. Put into an air-tight container and store in the refrigerator. Will last at least 3 weeks.

You can use cold water to soak the dates - however it will take several hours for them to soften.

This is a great ingredient that we add to many of our meals. Onion is sweet when cooked well.

Onion Jam

MAKES 2 CUPS

3 large finely sliced onions

2 tablespoons rice bran oil

4 tablespoons honey or date puree

1. Put all ingredients in a pot or pan on high heat and stir well for a couple of minutes until the moisture starts to come out.

2. Turn down the heat to low and let it bubble for around 30 minutes and eventually the onion will caramelise and become very sweet.

Add to almost any meal for amazing flavour and texture.

There are many ways to enjoy sweet foods without all of the processed sugars and flours that usually go with them.

Sweet Things

A great healthy ice-cream to try. At my cooking demonstrations this always impresses people as it tastes better than most expect. After one demonstration some of my helpers had a pile of mint left over and made a batch with about 10 times the amount of mint - it was divine - give it a try if you are brave!

Boysenberry Nice-Cream

1 cup raw cashew nuts

1 cup water

2 tablespoons honey or date puree

8 mint leaves

4 cups frozen boysenberries

1. Ideally you will need a food processor for this recipe (not a blender as they are for liquids).

2. Blend cashew nuts with about half of the water to form a smooth paste.

3. Add the rest of the ingredients and process until smooth.

4. You may need to add more water to keep it smooth but only just enough as you do not want it to become liquid.

5. Pour into serving glasses, garnish with a spare boysenberry and mint and serve immediately.

As an alternative, try this recipe with frozen strawberries, blueberries or mango.

Cashew Nuts

Cashew nuts are very creamy and great for giving things a thicker texture and great taste. Good in sweet things and stir fries. We generally use raw cashews at Revive.

This is a lovely cheesecake with no dairy or sugar. Just a clever combination of nuts, dried fruit and some frozen blueberries.

Blueberry & Cashew Cheesecake

BASE INGREDIENTS:

1 cup almonds

1 cup cashew nuts

1 cup dates

½ cup boiling water

FILLING INGREDIENTS:

2 cups cashew nuts

10 pitted dates

¼ teaspoon vanilla essence

pinch of salt

1 cup boiling water

TOPPING INGREDIENTS:

2 cups frozen blueberries

2 teaspoons arrowroot (or cornflour)

½ cup cold water

juice of half a lemon

1. Put dates and boiling water in a cup for 2 minutes to soften.

2. Combine with all other base ingredients into food processor and process until a clumpy texture. Do not over process. It should have some small pieces of cashews showing. You may need to add a little more water if it is too dry.

3. With a rubber spatula, press the base into a 25cm (10in) tart dish (the ones with the removable bottoms are best). Make sure you get a thick crust along the sides.

4. Soak filling dates in boiling water for 2 minutes and combine with all other filling ingredients in a food processor. Process until you have a very smooth cashew cream.

5. Pour out over the base and make level.

6. To make the topping, mix arrowroot, lemon juice and water in a cold small pot or frying pan.

7. Add blueberries and start heat (stirring well) until a gel has formed.

8. Pour blueberry topping over the cheesecake to complete. Use a fork to evenly distribute.

9. Refrigerate covered for several hours to help it firm up so it is easier to serve.

You will need a good food processor for this recipe to blend the nuts. It will not work with a blender or stick blender.

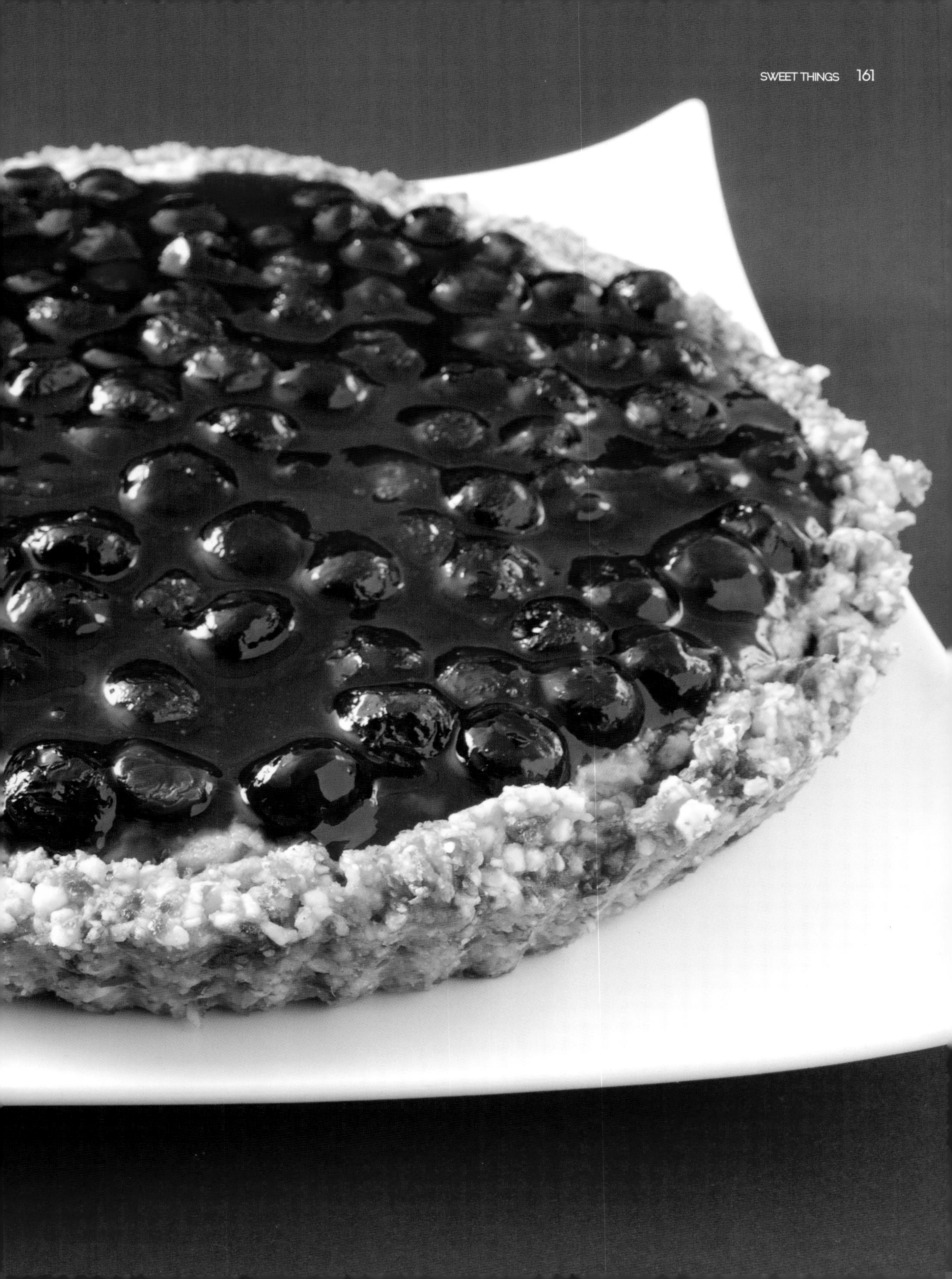

I discovered these one night on my quest to make a healthy hotcake. Buckwheat flour has a nice nutty taste that is not too intrusive, is a whole grain and is gluten free. What you put on top of hotcakes is what really makes them and this cashew and pear cream is divine and so easy.

Buckwheat Hotcakes with Cashew & Pear Cream

MAKES 12 SMALL
OR 5 LARGE

1¾ cups buckwheat flour

2 cups water

1 cup date puree or 4 tablespoons honey

2 large ripe bananas mashed

1 teaspoon ground coriander

½ teaspoon salt

3 tablespoons white sesame seeds

rice bran oil for frying

CASHEW & PEAR CREAM

400g (12oz) tinned pears (reserve juice)

1 cup raw cashew nuts

1. Mix all ingredients in a mixing bowl. No sifting required.

2. Adjust mixture with water if required to obtain pancake consistency.

3. Heat a large pan with a little oil.

4. Spoon mixture into pan, cooking around 3 minutes per side. You can choose to make a smaller hotcake size or larger pancake size.

5. In a blender (or use stick blender) mix up pears (without juice) and cashew nuts to make cashew & pear cream. Add a little pear juice if necessary to achieve a creamier consistency.

6. Serve with the cream, blueberries and a drizzle of honey.

You can easily make your own buckwheat flour with a food processor or coffee grinder. Just pop whole buckwheat in and blend until it is flour.

Blueberries

A delicious berry with an amazing colour. Keep a bag of frozen ones in your freezer. Great on breakfasts and in smoothies too.

We had this on at Revive for about a year - we alternated between apricot and plum slice. It is quick to make and no sugar or dairy so an ideal treat. Adding ginger brings a nice tang to this slice if you like it.

Apricot Oat Slice

MAKES 8 LARGE SLABS OR 16 SMALL SLABS

2 x 400g (12oz) tins apricots drained

3 cups date puree
(1½ cup water + 1½ cup dates blended)

½ cup rice bran oil

½ cup coconut shredded

1 cup rice flour

3 cups rolled oats
(finely cut variety)

½ cup sesame seeds

½ cup ground almonds

optional: 1 teaspoon ground ginger or 1 tablespoon ginger puree

1. Pre-heat your oven to 180°C (350°F).

2. Mix all ingredients (except apricots) in a large mixing bowl.

3. Select a baking tray approximately 200x300mm (8x12 in) and brush lightly with oil.

4. Press half of the mixture onto the baking tray.

5. Drain the apricots well and take out any stones. Crush with your fingers, place on top of the oat base and press down.

6. Sprinkle the remaining oat mix evenly on top of the apricot and press down evenly. Spray or brush a little oil on top to help stop it burning.

7. Bake for 30 minutes at 180°C (350°F) or until golden brown.

8. Cool and then cut into slabs with a serrated knife.

Try using canned black plums instead of apricots.

Rolled Oats

A great carbohydrate source and full of long lasting energy. Great for breakfasts and slices. Oats stick together well when moist so are great for these sorts of dishes.

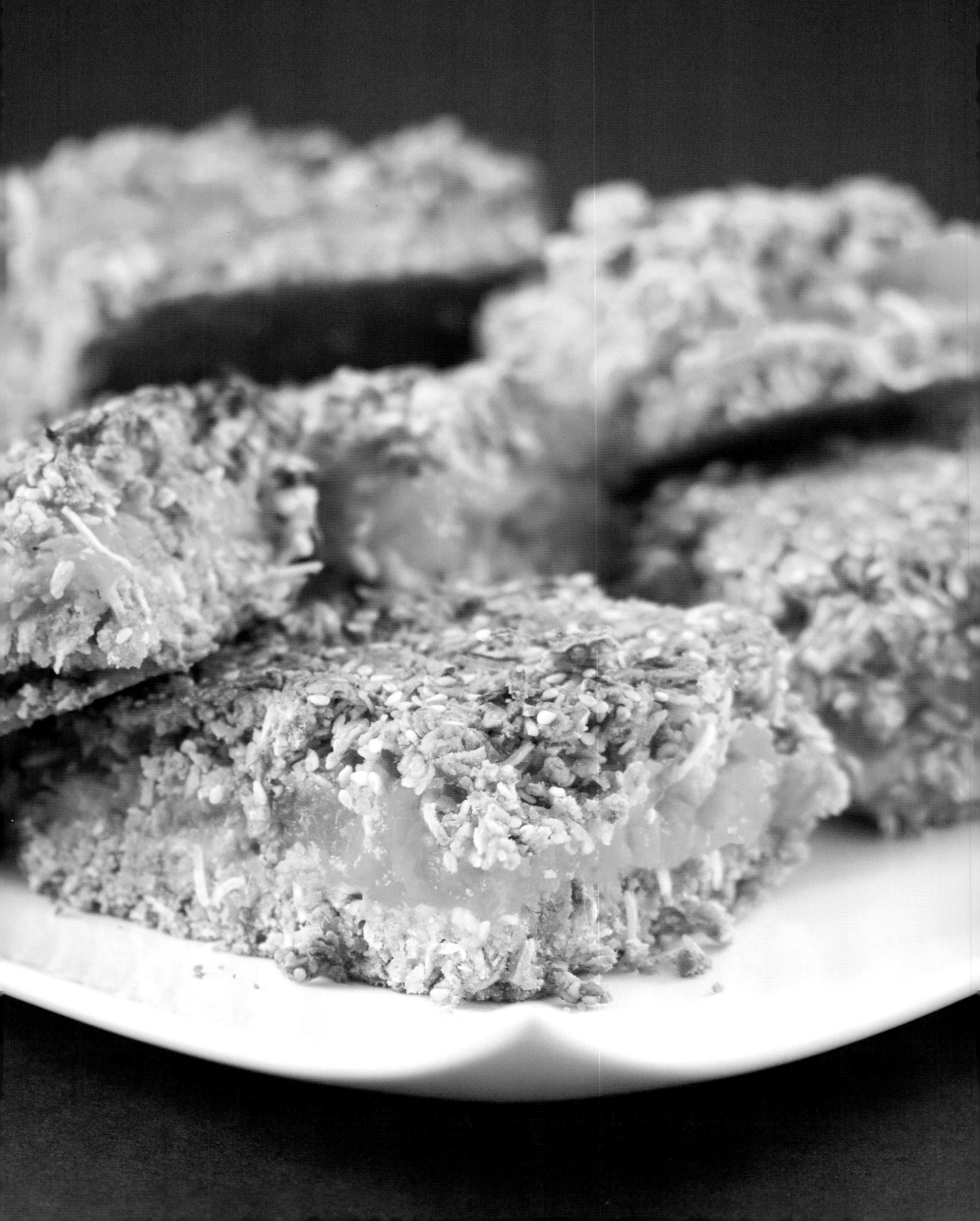

Simple, classic and tasty, this recipe can be used for many different flavours.

Blueberry Smoothie

MAKES 2 X 1 CUP SERVES

1 cup frozen blueberries

1 large ripe banana

1 cup soy or rice milk

2 tablespoons honey or date puree

optional: 1 cup ice

1. Put all ingredients into a blender and blend.

2. Serve immediately.

You can also use a stick blender to make smoothies however do not use it to blend ice as it will most likely break the blender.

Use the same recipe for strawberry or boysenberry smoothies.

I prefer one strong berry flavour per smoothie rather than a blend where the great berry flavours tend to get lost.

This is a different but tasty smoothie that people often request. Make sure you blend the dates well so they do not block up your straw.

Banana Date Smoothie

MAKES 2 X 1 CUP SERVES

10 dried dates

1 large ripe banana

1 cup soy or rice milk

1 cup ice

1. Put all ingredients in blender and blend. Make sure you blend the dates well.

2. Serve immediately.

You can put dates and some boiling water in the blender and let sit for a couple of minutes until soft before adding other ingredients. This process is not essential but it will be gentler on your blender and will not take as long to blend.

I found a rice pudding recipe in a cookbook one weekend. It looked delicious. However it contained very unhealthy ingredients. Butter, white rice, cream, milk and sugar made up 95% of it! Not really food if you ask me. So a friend challenged me to make a healthier version with more natural and wholesome ingredients. Here it is.

Boysenberry Rice Pudding

SERVES 4

1 cup short grain brown rice

1½ cups water

1½ cups rice milk or soy milk

2 tablespoons honey or date puree

¾ cup cashew nuts

½ cup water

½ teaspoon cinnamon

10 mint leaves finely chopped + some for garnish

2 cups frozen boysenberries plus 12 berries for garnish

1. Cook rice in water and milk (with lid on) for around 40 minutes or until it is sticky and liquid is gone.

2. Combine cashews and water. Blend with stick blender until smooth to make cashew cream.

3. Mix cooked rice, cashew cream, honey, cinnamon and mint.

4. Defrost (or heat lightly) boysenberries and blend well with stick blender. Drain off any excess liquid.

5. Layer in a glass. Boysenberry first, then rice, then boysenberry, then rice, then boysenberry. You will need less boysenberry than you think.

6. Add whole boysenberries and mint sprig for garnish.

7. Serve warm or chilled.

Boysenberries

These are my favourite berry. A strong flavour and vivid purple colour. Great in smoothies and desserts. Always keep a bag of frozen boysenberries in your freezer for an instant dessert, breakfast topping or smoothie.

This is the best possible breakfast you can have. It is full of high quality whole grains that will give you plenty of energy and nutrients to last through to lunchtime. There are 3 ways you can cook this. Pop this in the slow cooker and wake up to the smell of a cooked breakfast wafting through your house.

5 Grain Breakfast

FOR 2 LARGE OR
4 SMALL SERVINGS

1 cup 5 grain mix
- amaranth
- long grain brown rice (2 parts)
- quinoa
- buckwheat
- millet

4 cups boiling water

1 pinch salt

ADDITIONS

- soy or rice milk
- banana
- bee pollen
- berries (fresh or frozen)
- grated apple
- nuts
- dried fruit
- any other seasonal fruit
- ground flax seeds

1. Premix your grains and put in a container for easy use.

2. STOVE TOP: Combine all ingredients in a pot, lid on, bring to boil, turn down to low and simmer for 35 minutes.

3. SLOW COOKER (SLOW): Combine all ingredients (use cold water) and cook on low for around 5 hours.

4. SLOW COOKER (FAST): combine all ingredients in pot and cook on high for around 1½ hours.

5. Serve in a bowl and top with any combination of the additions listed.

6. The cooked 5 grain mix will be fine to refrigerate for a couple of days. So you can cook up 3 days supply at once to save time.

Add ½ cup dried fruit (sultanas, chopped dates, dried apricots) in the cooking process. They come out plump and juicy!

5 Grain Mix

You can mix any combination of grains together. My favourite is amaranth, rice, quinoa, buckwheat and millet. You can also add oats, bulghur wheat, whole wheat, sorghum and/or barley. If you change the mix you may need to adjust cooking times and water quantity slightly.

Make an amazing Swiss breakfast by spending a couple of minutes preparing the night before. This is a delicious breakfast as all of the ingredients combine together into a moreish mix, and the dried fruit becomes nice and juicy. The apple and sultanas give sweetness, so no need to add sugar!

Bircher Muesli

MAKES 3 X 1 CUP SERVES

1 cup fine oats (although whole oats will work fine)

¾ cup orange juice

½ cup soy or rice milk

¼ cup sultanas

¼ cup chopped nuts of your choice (I prefer cashews and almonds)

¼ cup yoghurt (optional)

1 small-medium sized apple grated

optional: seasonal fruit of your choice

1. Mix all ingredients together in a bowl, cover and put in refrigerator overnight.

2. Note that the mixture will appear to be too runny - however it will thicken.

3. In the morning all of the ingredients will have merged together. Simply give a quick stir and scoop into your bowl.

4. Sprinkle with fresh fruit and some sliced nuts. Passion fruit, blueberries and banana all work well.

This recipe is very flexible so do not stress if you are missing an ingredient - experiment to come up with your favourite combination. You want the liquid to be about double the quantity of oats.

Optional: add some linseeds (flax seeds) to the original mix. They will soften overnight and be quite edible and will give you all of the great omega health benefits.

Sultanas/Raisins

Sultanas (dried white grapes) and raisins (dried red grapes) are excellent to add to many sweet dishes and also many salads. A nice fresh burst of sweetness is great. They are also good when soaked as they swell up and become even juicier.

Never fear trying something new and getting outside your comfort zone. This is where life's greatest experiences are found. Give some new dishes a try with this Step-by-Step guide and you can create something you can call your own.

Step-by-Step

There are really only a handful of recipes in the world. There are just millions of variations and combinations. This Step-by-Step guide will help you create your own meals and learn the principles of cooking healthy.

In this section I have revealed how I think when creating a meal. Making a new dish is actually really simple, it is just combining different ingredients that go together and ensuring you have different types, colours and flavours.

Probably the most important part is when you finish the dish to taste it and check if it is awesome. And then going back and adding that "something else" to make it special. There is rarely a dish where I do not have to add something extra. Be prepared to critique your cooking and make changes as necessary.

I have also added some quick guides in the back for cooking grains, beans and lentils.

These guides are not an exact science, however they should give you an excellent starting point.

Step-by-Step Curry

Just keep firing ingredients into your favourite pot and you finish with a delicious meal!

Serve over brown rice (or other whole grain) and with a fresh salad. You can freeze most curries.

Rough guide: this will make around 4 - 6 large serves.

1 Base
saute in your favourite frying pan or pot until soft

2 Flavours
add the following - then quickly mix with the base

3 Liquid
now add these quickly and mix well before the flavours burn

---

1 Base

add all:

2 tablespoons oil
1 large onion, diced
3 cloves garlic, crushed

optional:

2 tablespoons garlic puree
1 stalk lemongrass, finely diced

optional:

1 large carrot, diced
2 stalks celery, diced

optional:

chilli crushed, chilli powder or pinch cayenne pepper

2 Flavours

choose 1:

Thai: 1 tablespoon red curry paste mixed with 1 cup hot water

Indian: 1 teaspoon each of ground cumin, turmeric, coriander
optional: garam masala

Asian: 3 tablespoons miso mixed with 1 cup water

Spanish: 1 tablespoon smoked paprika

Satay: 2 tablespoons peanut butter mixed with 1 cup hot water

3 Liquid

add all:

2 x 400g (12oz) tins tomatoes (blend with stick blender if they are not fine)

1 cup boiling water

choose 1:

2 tablespoons honey

4 tablespoons date puree

1 teaspoon agave nectar

add:

1 teaspoon salt

7,056,000
different
combinations

4 Veges

stir these in - do not over-cook and go for a range of contrasting colours

5 Protein

add these last - just need heating so do not over-mix and damage

6 Garnish

the finishing touch - again select contrasting colours

---

choose 3:

1 cup frozen peas, spinach or corn (do not pre-cook)

2 courgettes chopped

1 red or orange capsicum, roughly dice or julienne

3 cups pre-roasted potato, sweet potato or pumpkin - cubed

2 carrots - pre roasted - sliced

20 raw button mushrooms - halved

2 cups chopped broccoli or cauliflower

---

choose 1:

fresh or frozen tofu (firm), chopped into 1cm (½in) cubes

400g (12oz) can red kidney beans

400g (12oz) can chickpeas (garbanzo beans)

400g (12oz) can white beans

400g (12oz) can black turtle beans

choose 1:

half tin (200g/6oz) coconut cream

½ cup almonds or cashew nuts blended w 1 cup water

---

choose 1 or 2:

½ cup chopped parsley

½ cup chopped coriander

1 tablespoon white and/or black sesame seeds

½ cup pumpkin seeds

½ cup roasted peanuts, cashews or slivered almonds

1 tablespoon poppy seeds

1 small tin bamboo shoots

¼ cup cashew nuts

Step-by-Step Smoothie

The ultimate healthy sweet dessert. Smoothies are great in summer and you can make them in minutes.

Simply put all the ingredients in your blender, food processer or use a stick blender, then pour into a nice glass. They will not keep in the refrigerator so you do need to consume straight away.

Rough guide: this will make around 2 serves

1 Thickness
put in blender

2 Liquid
add to blender

3 Sweetness
add to blender

Thickness	Liquid	Sweetness
add: 1 large ripe banana (or for an even smoother texture use a frozen banana) optional: 1 cup ice (but do not use a stick blender with ice)	choose 1: 1 cup soy milk 1 cup rice milk 1 cup almond milk 1 cup apple juice 1 cup orange juice (you may need to add more depending on thickness)	optional - choose 1: 1 tablespoon honey 2 tablespoons date puree or 6 dates 1 peeled orange

201,600
different
combinations

4 Primary Flavour
add to blender

5 Extra Flavour
add to blender

6 Extras
add to blender

choose 1:

1 cup frozen boysenberries

1 cup frozen strawberries

1 cup frozen blueberries

1 can peaches with juice (unsweetened)

1 can pineapple with juice (unsweetened)

1 can apricots with juice (unsweetened)

optional - add 1 or 2:

1 drop vanilla essence

½ teaspoon ground coriander

4 sprigs mint

pinch cinnamon or nutmeg

optional - add 1 or 2:

½ cup rolled oats

½ cup cooked rice or quinoa

¼ cup cashews or almonds

1 tablespoon sesame seeds

1 tablespoon peanut butter/tahini

½ teaspoon bee pollen

1 teaspoon green barley powder

7 Check
for sweetness, flavour and viscosity and adjust if necessary

Step-by-Step Salad

Throw all your great ingredients into a big kitchen mixing bowl and use your hands to toss all the ingredients together. It is very exciting to feel the ingredients and flavours come together right in your hands.

Choose either carb, protein or vegetable salads. Or combine some or all, it is up to you!

Rough guide: this will make around 4 - 6 large serves

1 Carb
optional to add

optional - choose 1:

cooked brown rice

roasted potatoes, kumara, carrot or pumpkin

cooked quinoa

cooked bulghur wheat

cooked couscous (fine or Israeli)

cooked rice

cooked rice noodles

cooked wholemeal pasta (penne, fusilli, fettuccine, shells)

2 Protein
optional to add

optional - choose 1:

cooked french green (puy) lentils

400g (12oz) can red beans

400g (12oz) can white beans

400g (12oz) can black beans

400g (12oz) can black-eye beans

400g (12oz) can chickpeas (garbanzo beans)

3 Vegetable
choose a lettuce base or let the vegetables enhance the other ingredients

choose 1 or more:

mesclun lettuce

cos lettuce

baby or ripped spinach

finely sliced red & white cabbage

steamed broccoli or cauliflower

grated carrot

cubed tomatoes

cubed cucumber

roasted pumpkin and/or kumara (sweet potato)

102,960,000
different combinations

4 Dressing
moisture and flavour - you can also serve on the side

5 Extras
little bits of great taste - remember to use colours not already used if you can

6 Garnish
the finishing touch - again select contrasting colours

choose 1:

satay sauce

aioli

lemon juice or lemon dressing

chermoula dressing

balsamic vinegar

sweet chilli sauce

date puree or honey

pesto

honey mustard dressing

crushed chilli

miso paste mixed with water

choose 1 or 2:

olives

sultanas or raisins

feta cheese

croutons

sliced red onion

frozen corn or peas

spices

1 teaspoon smoked paprika

1 teaspoon curry powder

thai curry paste mixed w water

ginger puree

choose 1 or 2:

½ cup chopped parsley or other fresh herbs

1 tablespoon white and/or black sesame seeds

½ cup pumpkin seeds

1 tablespoon poppy seeds

¼ cup of cashew nuts

julienne beetroot strips

bean sprouts (mung/alfalfa)

chopped spring onions

shredded coconut

7 Check
for flavour and add a little salt or more ingredients if necessary

Step-by-Step *Stir Fry*

This is the quickest meal option you can make when you want dinner fast.

The key to a great stir fry is many different coloured vegetables combined with some amazing flavours.

Rough guide: this will make around 4 - 6 large serves

1 Base
saute in your favourite frying pan or wok until soft

2 Veges
stir these in - do not over-cook and go for a range of contrasting colours

3 Grains
stir in

Base

add all:

4 tablespoons oil
1 large onion diced
3 cloves garlic crushed

optional:

2 tablespoons ginger puree or finely chopped ginger

optional:

1 large carrot diced
2 stalks celery diced
1 medium red onion roughly chopped

Veges

choose at least 3:

1 cup frozen peas, spinach or corn (do not pre-cook)

2 courgettes (zucchini) chopped

1 red or orange capsicum - roughly diced or julienne

2 cups pre-roasted potato, sweet potato or pumpkin - cubed

10 raw button mushrooms - halved

2 cups chopped broccoli or cauliflower

any other vegetables in season

Grains

choose 1:

2 cups pre-cooked quinoa

2 cups pre-cooked brown rice (short or long grain)

2 cups pre-cooked buckwheat

59,400,000
different combinations

4 Flavours
stir in

5 Protein
add these last - just need heating so do not over-mix and damage

6 Garnish
the finishing touch - select contrasting colours

---

add all:

½ teaspoon salt

2 tablespoons honey or date puree

choose 1:

4 tablespoon soy sauce or tamari

1 teaspoon Thai curry paste mixed with ¼ cup water

1 tablespoon Indian curry paste

2 teaspoons smoked paprika

½ teaspoon each of ground turmeric, coriander and cumin

---

choose 1:

fresh or frozen tofu (firm), chopped into 1cm (½in) cubes

400g (12oz) can red kidney beans

400g (12oz) can chickpeas (garbanzo beans)

400g (12oz) can white beans

400g (12oz) can black turtle beans

any other beans

use your own freshly cooked or frozen beans if you can

---

choose 1 or 2:

sprinkle of black or white sesame seeds

chopped fresh herbs

juice of 1 lemon squeezed over

roasted cashew nuts or almonds

finely chopped peanuts

large spoon of hummus

freshly made tomato sauce

sprinkle of cayenne pepper

7 Check
for saltiness, flavour, sweetness & texture and adjust if necessary

Step-by-Step Fritters

These are so easy to make and there are so many combinations you can choose from.
When making fritters I make a test one first to check flavour, the heat of the pan and that everything sticks together.

Combine all items in a bowl and cook in a hot lightly oiled frying pan – around 2 minutes each side.

Rough guide: this will make around 10 medium fritters to serve 3 - 4 people.

1 Flour
start with a mixing bowl

2 Liquid
add to bowl and mix well with a fork

3 Base
stir into mix

1 Flour

choose 1:

1½ cups wholemeal flour

1½ cups chickpea (besan) flour

2 Liquid

choose 1:

½ cup water

½ cup soy/rice milk

also add:

1 teaspoon salt

optional:

2 tablespoons date puree or 1 tablespoon honey

2 tablespoons sweet chilli sauce

3 Base

optional:

1 pre-cooked large diced or sliced onion

optional:

2 cloves garlic - crushed

70,560
different combinations

4 **Key Item**
stir into mix

5 **Flavour**
add these little bits of great taste

6 **Garnish**
add contrasting colours after cooking is completed

choose 1 or more:

400g (120oz) whole kernal corn or 2 cups frozen

3 courgettes (zucchini) chopped finely

2 carrots grated

2 potatoes - steamed & grated

2 apples grated

choose at least 1:

1 teaspoon curry powder

½ cup chopped fresh coriander or parsley

1 teaspoon ground cumin

1 tablespoon sesame oil

1 teaspoon Indian or Thai curry paste

choose 1:

freshly chopped chives

chopped fresh herbs

black or white sesame seeds

honey or sweet chilli sauce drizzled over them

optional dipping sauce:

sweet chilli sauce

pineapple or tomato salsa

chutney or tomato sauce

aioli or other dressing

7 **Check**
for flavour, saltiness and texture and adjust if necessary

Quick Guide Cooking Grains

Whole grains are high in fibre and nutrients. I prefer cooking on the stove top.
Most grains yield approximately double their dry volume.

1. Boil water in your kettle - this will help cut time off the cooking process.
2. Put the required ratio of boiling water and grains into a pot at highest heat with the lid on.
3. Bring to the boil and then turn down and simmer (just bubbling). This is usually around ¼ heat setting.
4. Simmer for the required amount of time or until soft. If not quite cooked you can leave to sit with lid on for another 10 minutes.
5. When the water reduces, steam vents will appear in the grains that assist with cooking. Do not stir as you will interrupt it.

		water	simmer
Long Grain Brown Rice - 1 cup A great staple grain that I use most.		2 cups	30 minutes

		water	time
Short/Medium Grain Brown Rice - 1 cup Great for sticky rice salads.		3 cups	40 minutes

		water	simmer
Bulghur Wheat - 1 cup Depending on the size the time may vary.		2 cups	20 minutes

		water	simmer
Buck Wheat - 1 cup A nice soft grain. Just needs a lot of flavour.		2 cups	20 minutes

		water	let sit
Fine Couscous - 1 cup Don't cook. Just mix with boiling water and stir.		1 cup	5 minutes

		water	simmer
Quinoa - 1 cup The perfect quick cooking grain. High in protein.		2 cups	12 minutes

Quick Guide Cooking Beans

Beans are high in protein. Cooking your own beans is easy with some planning and you will save a lot of money.

These times are very approximate as the cooking time will vary significantly depending on the age and size of the bean.

1. Soak overnight (or at least 6 hours) in water (3 times as much water as beans).

2. Drain water and rinse in a colander or sieve.

3. Put fresh boiling water and beans into a pot and bring to boil. Simmer (just bubbling) on high heat for time specified or until soft.

4. Rinse under cold water in a colander or sieve.

5. Use straight away or put in refrigerator. Can be frozen and will defrost quickly under hot water.

		water	time
Chickpeas (Garbanzo Beans) - 1 cup Our most used, favourite and delicious bean.		6 cups	40 minutes
Red Kidney Beans - 1 cup Good all purpose bean - great colour.		6 cups	60 minutes
Small White (Navy) Beans - 1 cup Good soft bean to cook.		6 cups	60 minutes
Black (Turtle) Beans - 1 cup Nice in hotpots and salads for contrast.		6 cups	30 minutes
Large Lima (Butter) Beans - 1 cup Amazing in salads.		6 cups	60 minutes
Black Eyed Beans - 1 cup Nice in stews and hotpots.		6 cups	30 minutes
Pinto Beans - 1 cup Great all round bean.		6 cups	50 minutes

Quick Guide Cooking Lentils

Lentils are high in protein and great in almost any savoury dish.

1. Lentils do not need soaking (except whole urid).

2. Bring to the boil with the amounts of water indicated below and then turn down to simmer.

3. Cook with lid off for the approximate cooking times or until soft. Be careful as they can burn if water runs out.

4. Do not add salt until the end as this will inhibit the cooking process. Water will usually be used up but if not, drain.

5. Freeze any leftovers.

		water	time
Red Lentils - 1 cup Fast cooking and staple pantry item.		3 cups	10 minutes
Yellow (Toor Dahl) Lentils - 1 cup Like red lentils but a different texture and flavour.		3 cups	15 minutes
French Green (Puy) Lentils - 1 cup Cook until just soft. Retains shape.		4 cups	40 minutes
Urid (Black) Lentils Split - 1 cup Soak overnight. Whole will take longer to cook.		6 cups	50 minutes
Brown (Crimson) Lentils - 1 cup Great in lasagnes and casseroles. Nice with sage.		3 cups	30 minutes
Laird (Brown/Green) Lentils - 1 cup Often called brown lentils. Need a lot of flavour.		3 cups	30 minutes

Recipe Index